OSPREY AIRCRAFT OF THE ACES® • 41

American Volunteer Group Colours and Markings

SERIES EDITOR: TONY HOLMES

OSPREY AIRCRAFT OF THE ACES® • 41

American Volunteer Group Colours and Markings

Terrill Clements

OSPREY
PUBLISHING

Front cover
On Christmas Day 1941, more than 150 fighters and bombers of the Japanese Imperial Army Air Force attacked Rangoon and nearby Allied installations. Opposing them were 13 Tomahawks of the American Volunteer Group's Third ('Hell's Angels') Pursuit Squadron and 14 Brewster Buffaloes of the Royal Air Force's No 67 Sqn. Ex-Army Air Corps pilot Bill Reed scrambled with his flight at 1115 hrs, and duly orbited uneventfully for 30 minutes before finally intercepting the enemy. After skirmishing with the escorting fighters and making a head-on pass on the bombers, who were by then returning to base, he turned in pursuit and joined his Flight Leader, Parker Dupouy, in a dogfight with three fighters. Unable to get into a good position from which to open fire, both men dove out to escape the more manoeuvrable Japanese aeroplanes. Reed later wrote in his diary;

'By now we were 140-150 miles across the gulf from Rangoon. We started back across the Gulf at 17,000 ft, and had only gone about 30 miles out off the shore of Moulmein when we spotted three Model 0s (Ki-43 'Oscars') in a V-formation below us, apparently headed home. We dropped down on their tails and surprised them. Dupouy was following me as I picked out the right-hand wingman. I fired from about 50 yards and Dupouy fired behind me and to the right. The Jap exploded right in my face. I pulled sharply up to the right to avoid hitting him, and Dupouy pulled up to the left. In doing so, his right wing clipped the other wingman's ship right at the wing root, and the Jap spun into the Gulf too. The leader got the drop on me as I went by him, and after managing to meet him almost head-on in one turn, and losing ground in the next, I dove away. I climbed back to get at him again, but no one was to be seen. I was damn low on gas, so I decided to head straight over the Gulf in the general direction of Rangoon'

Reed landed at about 1430 hrs, finding that both the airfield and Rangoon had suffered heavy damage. Dupouy reported that 'four feet of my right wing and one half of my right aileron were knocked off, however my aeroplane flew for three-quarters of an hour' before he successfully dodged the bomb craters while landing at Mingaladon at 140 mph. Reed and Dupouy's victims were Sgt Shigekatsu Wakayama and Lt Hiroshi Okuyama of the 64th Sentai. The AVG lost two aircraft that day, not including Dupouy's badly damaged fighter, while No 67 Sqn had four Buffaloes shot down and four pilots killed. The Allies claimed 25 Japanese aircraft in what was the largest air battle of the Pacific War up to that time (*Cover artwork by Iain Wyllie*)

First published in Great Britain in 2001 by Osprey Publishing
Elms Court, Chapel Way, Botley, Oxford, OX2 9LP

© 2001 Osprey Publishing Limited

ISBN 1 84176 224 5

Edited by Tony Holmes
Page design by Tony Truscott
Cover artwork by Iain Wyllie
Aircraft profiles by Jim Laurier
Scale drawings by Mark Styling
Origination by Grasmere Digital Imaging, Leeds, UK
Printed through Bookbuilders, Hong Kong

00 01 02 03 04   10 9 8 7 6 5 4 3 2 1

EDITOR'S NOTE
To make this best-selling series as authoritative as possible, the Editor would be interested in hearing from any individual who may have relevant photographs, documentation or first-hand experiences relating to the world's elite pilots and units, and the aircraft they flew, in the various theatres of war. Any material used will be credited to its original source. Please write to Tony Holmes at 10 Prospect Road, Sevenoaks, Kent, TN13 3UA, Great Britain, or by e-mail at: tony.holmes@osprey-jets.freeserve.co.uk

For a catalogue of all Osprey Publishing titles please contact us at:

Osprey Direct UK, PO Box 140, Wellingborough, Northants NN8 4ZA, UK
E-mail: **info@ospreydirect.co.uk**

Osprey Direct USA, c/o Motorbooks International, 729 Prospect Ave, PO Box 1, Osceola, WI 54020, USA
E-mail: **info@ospreydirectusa.com**

Or visit our website: **www.ospreypublishing.com**

CONTENTS

PREFACE

I n this modest-sized volume I hope to provide some details about the aircraft and operations of the American Volunteer Group (AVG), or 'Flying Tigers' – the sort of small but important matters that are so often glossed over in more conventional narratives. The broader context of these things could not be ignored of course, but much had to be left out of this short work. Nonetheless, readers who think there is nothing new to be learned about this legendary unit should still find a few items of interest.

Colours, markings and equipment details are not the most momentous historical subjects, but I have tried to approach these things in a sensible, reasoned way, relying on photographs, first person accounts and records, and the recollections of some of the men who were there. But at this late date much evidence is lost, and some details, such as complete airframe histories, defy resolution. Any errors or omissions here are of course my own.

A number of AVG veterans – some of the men who really 'wrote' this work – were interviewed for this book. They were: Frank Andersen (Jacobson), 1st Sqn Crew Chief; George Bailey, 2nd Sqn Crew Chief; Chuck Baisden, 3rd Sqn Armorer; Charles R Bond, Jr, 1st Sqn Vice Leader; Keith Christensen, 3rd Sqn Armorer; Paul J Greene, 3rd Sqn pilot; David Lee 'Tex' Hill, 2nd Sqn Leader; Ken Jernstedt, 3rd Sqn Flight Leader; Robert 'Buster' Keeton, 2nd Sqn pilot; Robert Layher, 2nd Sqn pilot; Frank Losonsky, 3rd Sqn Crew Chief; Charles Mott, Group Adjutant and 2nd Sqn pilot; Joe Poshefko, 3rd Sqn Armorer; Rolland Richardson, Group Communications; Richard Rossi, 1st Sqn pilot; Leo J Schramm, 3rd Sqn Crew Chief; Edward L Stiles, 3rd Sqn Crew Chief; Irving Stolet, 3rd Sqn Crew Chief; George Tyrell, 2nd Sqn Crew Chief; and Peter Wright, 2nd Sqn Flight Leader. Many thanks to all of them for so generously sharing their time, recollections and priceless photographs.

Also, a thank-you to Erik Shilling, 3rd Sqn pilot, for taking the time to respond to my e-mail queries. I would especially like to acknowledge the invaluable assistance of the late Robert T Smith, 3rd Squadron Flight Leader, who inspired me years ago with his wonderful photos and patient answers to my many questions. His son, Brad Smith, generously provided access to 'R T's' entire photograph collection, and without his assistance this book would really not have been possible. I am also greatly indebted to David L Armstrong, Mark Burken, Jinx Rodger and Carl Molesworth for their help with many of the photos. I have also benefited from the contributions and insights of Ben Levario, Dr Ted Brown, Bruce Fraites and Russ Fahey. Many thanks to you all, and my apologies to anyone I have forgotten.

Many published sources were also relied on. Space limitations preclude a complete listing, but the single most useful collection of photographs is found in Larry M Pistole's *Pictorial History of the Flying Tigers*. The two best pilot's accounts are Charles Bond's *A Flying Tiger's Diary* and Robert T Smith's *Tale of A Tiger*. The best accounts by AVG ground personnel are Charles N Baisden's *Flying Tiger To Air Commando*, Frank Losonsky's *Flying Tiger: A Crew Chief's Story*, Robert M Smith's *With Chennault In China: A Flying Tiger's Diary*, and Leo J Schramm's *Leo The Tiger*.

Three video documentaries provided invaluable colour and black and white film – *Fei Hu: The Story of the Flying Tigers*, *The Real Flying Tigers*, and *Flying Tigers and the Fourteenth Air Force Story*. Those with access to the internet should also consult 'The Official Flying Tigers Home Page', 'Aeroplanes and Pilots of World War II', 'Nothing New About Death' and 'George Burgard's Flying Tiger Days' for additional first-person accounts, primary materials and ongoing discussions of the remarkable AVG. I hope that this book makes some small contribution to this body of work.

Terrill Clements
Seattle, Washington
September 2001

FORMATION OF THE AVG

'**W**e are making shark heads out of the front end', wrote Robert T Smith in his Collins Indian Royal Diary on Tuesday, 18 November 1941. 'Looks mean as hell'. Smith was a Flight Leader in the Third Pursuit Squadron of the American Volunteer Group, the 'civilian' unit that would soon be known throughout the world as the 'Flying Tigers'. The artwork had started appearing on the Group's Tomahawk fighters just one day prior to this diary entry.

Smith could not have known during those hectic days at Toungoo, Burma, that the striking shark heads that AVG personnel were painting on its aeroplanes would become one of the most famous visual images in aviation history, or that the 'civilian' AVG would itself gain legendary status for its unparalleled successes in the bleak and desperate early months of the Pacific War. Surprisingly, however, little accurate information about the markings and other details of these shark-headed Curtiss fighters has appeared since the group ended operations on 4 July 1942.

The American Volunteer Group, and its equipment, were products of a desperate and dangerous time. A war of savage brutality raged in China following Japanese aggression at the Marco Polo Bridge in July 1937. By 1940 the Chinese were in a desperate position, with only the new Burma Road remaining as a line of supply. And as the news from Asia worsened, Japan joined the German-Italian Axis and occupied French Indochina.

The Chinese desperately needed help, and pressed the Roosevelt Administration for military aid. But American neutrality laws limited direct aid to the agricultural and economic credits provided China through the Universal Trading Corporation. And because China was without a merchant marine, and effectively besieged anyway, 'cash and carry' requirements precluded Chinese purchases from American firms.

During the fateful summer of 1940 matters continued to worsen, and bowing to Japanese pressure, the British closed the Burma side of the road for several months. With increasing desperation, Nationalist Chinese representatives in the US began to meet secretly with officials of the Roosevelt Administration to discuss drastic aid measures that took the form of an American-manned air unit to be led by Claire Chennault, an ex-Army Air Corps officer and now air advisor to Generalissimo Chiang Kai-shek.

An agreement was finally reached, and on 23 December 1940 President Roosevelt signed a secret order that would create a covert American-manned Chinese air unit as a part of the Curtiss-affiliated Central Aircraft Manufacturing Company (CAMCO).

CAMCO had been assembling and maintaining Curtiss aircraft for the Nationalist Chinese government since 1933, and had a good facility on the Burma Road at Loiwing, in China. Curtiss, then the largest manufacturer of aircraft in the United States, was busy mass-producing Tomahawk fighters for both the US Army and America's friends abroad. One hundred of these were to be diverted to China and paid for by the Universal Trading Corporation with money actually intended for general economic stabilisation loans. US Navy, Army and Marine Corps pilots and ground crewmen would be secretly recruited to man this so-called 'American Volunteer Group'.

They would be given special discharges to work for CAMCO in its 'aircraft manufacturing, operating and repair' business, with the proviso that when their one-year contracts ended they would be able to return to their respective Services without loss of time in grade. Pay would be extremely generous to encourage volunteers for this unusual and dangerous venture. But funding a covert military operation through the Universal Trading Corporation was politically risky in the isolationist climate of the times. So another shadowy corporation operating out of the Chinese embassy, China Defense Supplies, became the financing cover for the operation. After passage of the Lend-Lease Act in March 1941, funds would flow more openly.

Strictly speaking, this was the *First* American Volunteer Group. Two additional groups, one each of bombers and fighters, were also planned as part of a clandestine 'Special Air Unit' that would not only provide top cover for China's supply line, but conduct an ambitious – and incredibly risky – undeclared air war against Japan itself.

In July 1941 President Roosevelt issued secret orders to establish the volunteer bomber group. An embargo on oil sales to Japan was announced at that time as well, and we now know that this action set in motion Japan's decision to extend its war to the United States and other Western powers. But at the time of Japan's attack at Pearl Harbor on 7 December, only the First American Volunteer Group was in place. Plans for the other units were immediately scrapped. The original mission, to protect the Burma Road, would also change as events unfolded.

PERSONNEL AND EQUIPMENT

Chennault set to work in early 1941 to obtain the Tomahawks and other equipment the AVG would need, his 'shopping' hampered by the secret and irregular nature of the operation. Meanwhile, CAMCO recruiters began making the rounds of US military installations. They wanted groundcrewmen and pilots who had experience with fighters – especially the P-40 – but as the time for deployment shortened, standards became more flexible.

Robert 'Buster' Keeton was a flying boat pilot in VP-13, and he recalls that a recruiter came to his base three times. At first he wouldn't even talk to flying boat pilots, saying he only wanted pilots with fighter experience. A few weeks later he was willing to consider dive-bomber and torpedo-bomber pilots. On the third visit the CAMCO man would consider any pilot who was interested, and Keeton signed up. Second Squadron pilot Robert Layher was also piloting flying boats when he heard about the CAMCO recruiters. Dinner and a bottle of Scotch convinced the CAMCO man to sign him up, him, and several others as well. They were among the last pilots to join.

Everyone had his own reasons for joining the AVG. Peter Wright, a dive-bomber pilot flying 'neutrality patrols' in VS-42, was feeling like

AVG pilot Allen 'Bert' Christman looks dapper despite the stifling heat, while AVG Tomahawks are assembled in the background at Mingaladon Aerodrome, near Rangoon, in the Autumn of 1941. Christman worked as a comic strip artist before joining the Navy, where he was assigned to VS-41 aboard the USS *Ranger*. In June 1941 he resigned along with friends Tex Hill and Ed Rector to join the AVG, a job that in his words had 'a real purpose'. AVG Third Squadron pilot Robert T Smith met him on the trip overseas, and described him as quiet but friendly – 'a wonderful guy'. Christman was a good pilot and made the transition to Tomahawks quickly. He also continued his drawing, and apparently lobbied for the 'Panda Bear' mascot for the Second Squadron. He also made daily cartoons of current events called 'Logan's Log', but his best-known AVG cartoons were pilot caricatures he painted on some of the squadron's aeroplanes. These were probably the first individualised 'nose art' done by an American in World War 2 (*David Armstrong*)

'a boxer with no one to box'. The AVG would provide some sort of action, although he wasn't quite sure what it would be. He was also planning to get married, and joining the AVG would allow him to save money and probably avoid him the disruption of sea duty when his contract ended. The money was certainly good, as was the prospect of flying the latest American fighter aeroplane. And he thought he could do a little good helping the Chinese resist Japanese aggression.

Others, like Marine pilot Ken Jernstedt, also felt sympathy for the plight of the Chinese, but in any event the AVG was obviously an adventure that would be much more interesting than peacetime military service. Some joined simply to put some distance between them and their present situations and concerns. Groundcrewmen in particular stood to receive an immense pay increase – no small matter for men who had lived through the Depression in working-class families.

Keith Christensen was a First Class Ordnanceman in the Navy, and he thought the pay offered by the AVG was 'out of this world'. Irving Stolet was a welding specialist in the Army Air Corps when he was offered $350 per month to join the AVG as a Crew Chief. He wasn't told much about the job he was getting himself into, and didn't even know where he would be going, but he would have 'gone to hell for that kind of money'.

Chennault, with much-needed diplomatic backing, made arrangements with reluctant British military authorities in Burma to use Kyedaw airfield, near Toungoo, as the AVG's training base. The 'blacktop' airstrip itself was too short and narrow, and facilities were crude – particularly for operations during the seemingly endless monsoon season. But a base in then-neutral colonial Burma would not be subject to Japanese attack as a field in China would be. It was also conveniently located on the Burma Railway line 170 miles north of Rangoon, and 300 miles south of Lashio, the southern terminus of the Burma Road itself.

From Lashio the Road followed an ancient trade route 700 miles north through incredibly difficult terrain to Kunming, China, where the AVG's headquarters and main base of operations would be located.

At Rangoon, Commonwealth forces occupied the best base in the region at Mingaladon Aerodrome. In the coming months the AVG would get to know that field well. They would also operate from another British field at Magwe, about 80 miles north-west of Toungoo, among other smaller fields in northern Burma. And as the ground war went from bad to worse in the Spring of 1942, AVG operations would retire further north to the CAMCO field just over the Chinese border at Loiwing, then further up the Burma Road to Chinese fields at Baoshan, Yunnan-yi and Mengzi. The AVG would also utilise about 20 other forward staging, refuelling and dispersal fields in Burma and China.

CAMCO personnel arrived in Rangoon in late May 1941 to start preparations for the operation. These included Allison engine technician Walt Pentecost and test pilot Byron Glover. Pentecost was the technical 'advance man' in charge of supervising the uncrating and assembly of the aeroplanes. He had been signed up by yet another firm affiliated with CAMCO, the Intercontinent Company. Additional personnel were borrowed from CAMCO's operations at Loiwing. Waiting for them on the Rangoon docks was the first shipment of Curtiss model H81-A-2 Tomahawk fighter aeroplanes.

The AVG's fighters were taken in three separate batches from Curtiss production lines – 36 were shipped in January 1941 and arrived in Rangoon in May, 33 were shipped in February and arrived in June, and the final 31 aeroplanes were shipped in March and arrived in July. Curtiss records refer to the AVG's aeroplanes as H81-A-3 models, but in fact the sole surviving data plate from one of these fighters is marked 'H81-A-2'. The AVG also obtained 50 spare Allison V-1710-C15 (-33) engines. Wing guns, optical gunsights and radio equipment were not supplied by Curtiss. These were discreetly obtained by CAMCO from other sources.

The first substantial group of AVG personnel – all groundcrewmen – arrived in Burma on 28 July 1941 on the *President Pierce*, and the AVG was officially established on 1 August. Altogether, 99 pilots signed up under original contracts with CAMCO. Of this number, 33 were from the Army Air Corps, 59 were from the Navy and seven had flown in the Marines.

Some 37 pilots and 86 more groundcrewmen arrived in Burma on 15 August after crossing the Pacific on the Dutch ship *Jaegersfontein*. The next contingent of pilots and groundcrewmen arrived via the *Bloemfontein* on 15 September, and a further six pilots arrived on 10 October after crossing on the *Zaandam* and taking other transportation overland to Rangoon. The *Klipfontein* arrived at Rangoon on 29 October with ten pilots, while 26 more arrived on 12 November, having shipped aboard the *Boschfontein*. The final contingent – four AVG pilots and some instructors for the Chinese Air Force – shipped over on another trip by the *Zaandam*, and finally arrived on 25 November. A further ten ex-USAAC flight instructors at the Chinese Nationalist flight school at Yunnan-yi would also join the AVG in early 1942 when training operations ended there.

To his dismay, Chennault found that only 12 of the 99 pilots had any experience with the Tomahawk prior to joining the AVG, and about half of the rest had no fighter experience at all. The result of this was a longer than planned training period, and much wastage of equipment, and Chennault sent at least one strongly worded message to CAMCO about the practices of their recruiters. Clearly, however, some very well qualified men were signed up as well, and many of the pilots who had never flown a fighter before did a fine job despite their lack of experience. Significantly, the groundcrew personnel were particularly well qualified for their jobs, although some had no prior experience with Tomahawks or liquid-cooled Allison engines.

NINETY-NINE TOMAHAWKS

Walt Pentecost's team was ready to test-fly the first of the assembled Tomahawks at Mingaladon Aerodrome on 12 June. Yet by 15 August, when the first pilots began arriving, only three Tomahawks had been delivered to Kyedaw airfield, and three more were ready for collection. Deliveries increased rapidly after that though, with 22 aeroplanes being delivered in August, 21 in September, 29 in October and 27 in November. The last Tomahawk arrived at Toungoo on 28 November 1941.

Of the 100 fighters shipped to Burma, two airframes were found to be so badly damaged or deficient upon uncrating that the best parts of each were ultimately combined to make one operational aircraft. Thus, the

This Bert Christman snapshot of future Second Squadron Leader David Lee 'Tex' Hill provides a glimpse of the living quarters at Toungoo while the AVG trained there in 1941 (*David Armstrong*)

AVG had available to it a total of 99 Tomahawks. It would operate with this equipment until late March 1942, when the first P-40Es arrived from USAAF stocks in West Africa.

The AVG's Tomahawks differed somewhat from the airframes being shipped to Commonwealth forces from the same production lines – a fact reflected in factory photos of cockpit detail changes captioned 'H-81-A-2 (China)'. In fact the AVG's Tomahawks were not themselves identical in all details, perhaps due to incremental changes made on production lines then undergoing the greatest expansion in US aviation history. This may also explain Curtiss's use of the H81-A-3 designation for these aeroplanes in its billing paperwork. But specific technical details have been a source of much confusion through the years.

The AVG's Tomahawks were neither true P-40Bs nor P-40Cs, although AVG personnel themselves used both designations in everyday communications. Weight and performance figures for these machines were probably close to those typically given for the P-40B model however. Indeed, when these aeroplanes were taken over by the Army Air Forces in July 1942, many were stencilled with P-40B data blocks.

They certainly could not accommodate the 52-gallon belly tank that the C-model could carry, and there were other aspects of the fuel systems, instrumentation and general details that differed from both the P-40C and P-40B models built for the Army Air Corps, and from other H81-A-2 airframes for that matter.

Curtiss apparently cobbled together the allotments with something less than fastidious quality control as well. Third Squadron Crew Chief Frank Losonsky recalled that fellow Crew Chief Carl Quick even had to deal with some aeroplanes that had the throttle action reversed in the French manner, and he had to install the armour plate in two of the Tomahawks he worked on.

All the aeroplanes were factory-equipped with a 'ring and post' gunsight, but CAMCO had to acquire model N-3A optical gunsights for installation in Burma. These were designed to be mounted on the cockpit floor, projecting the sighting 'pipper' onto a separate reflector or combining glass mounted in the pilot's line of sight on the windscreen. This arrangement had been less than satisfactory on Army P-40s, and it presented even more problems for the AVG, as Group Adjutant Charles Mott found. First, the windscreen lacked the mounting holes for the reflector, and AVG mechanics had no equipment to drill them!

It was some time before AVG Tomahawks had any official markings on them other than the small serial numbers on the fin which was added as they were uncrated. This shot, taken at Kyadaw airfield near Toungoo, probably in early September 1941, shows an informal attempt to improve recognition. Note the hasty '15' (and less visible '3rd') marked on the tail of the aeroplane at right (P-8115). That's Crew Chief Frank Losonsky on the bike (*Frank Losonsky*)

To make the situation more complicated, the AVG's Tomahawks were also equipped with a thick bullet-resistant glass shield mounted behind the windscreen. Second, the ring portion of the sighting reticule – which had to match the likely target's wingspan at the range to which the guns were boresighted – was the wrong size for the Japanese 'Model 0s' that Chennault expected his unit to face. Of course no one in Burma had the precision equipment to fashion new ones.

Mott thought the reflector problem could be solved by simply using the armour glass itself as the reflector for the sight. Experiments revealed however that a confusing double image – one on each surface of the armour glass – resulted. Mott found that an application of light oil on one side eliminated one of the reflections, and demonstrated this to Chennault, who was dubious of the value of optical sights anyway.

But this would be a temporary solution at best, and Mott figured that a transparent resin such as Canada Balsam would do the job, but also harden to make a permanent fix. Nothing like that was available in Toungoo, however, and on 6 October Mott prevailed on a reluctant Chennault to send him to Rangoon to look there. None could be found there either, so the only solution was to devise some way to mount the combining glass provided with the optical sight.

Mott decided that a bracket that would bolt onto the frame of the armour glass would do the trick, and he spent an afternoon making a s uitable design drawing. He then searched for a Rangoon firm that could quickly make 100 of them. Several British-owned companies could do the work, but were not in any hurry to do so. One (probably the firm of Lawrence & Mayo) finally agreed after Mott told them he would go to the RAF and get the necessary priority. By October 10 they were done and next day Mott loaded them into a Tomahawk and flew back to Toungoo. Crew Chief Joe Gasdick helped him mount one for testing, although working out the necessary fine adjustments took much longer.

On October 14 Mott wrote in his diary that he had worked all day on 'the blooming sight' and 'the whole thing has been a headache'. But the adjustment process was sorted out, and soon the armourers were adept at installing and boresighting with them.

The reticule problem required a similarly creative solution. The reticules were made of glass, with a coating of black paint. The sighting pattern cast by the light shining through the reticule consisted simply of lines cut through the paint to the glass. Mott warmed them up over the chimney of a kerosene reading lamp until the paint was soft. Then, using a circle template made by drilling a piece of sheet metal, he scribed new circles of the correct diameter with a needle.

The resulting images were not always perfect of course, and a few pilots complained that the rings were 'ragged' or not accurately centred. Mott referred them to his 'quality control department', whose standard reply was 'if you don't like it, scratch it yourself'. But, as the Army had found out earlier, this type of sighting arrangement presented problems even when properly set up. Armorer Chuck Baisden notes that every time a pilot 'pulled himself out of the cockpit he would throw the sight off' since the armour glass was attached to the pilot's grab handle. And while Mott designed the bracket with setscrews to keep it in proper alignment, engine/airframe vibration could throw it off as time went on because of

Bert Christman poses for a snapshot in front of Tomahawk '71' at Toungoo in the Autumn of 1941. Note the colour demarcation at the wing root – evidence of a factory-applied paint job. Christman was considered one of the AVG's better pilots during training. He got his first chance for action on 10 December when he and Ed Rector escorted Group Photo Officer Erik Shilling on the first wartime mission of the group. Christman was eager to get into action, and he got ample opportunities when the Second Squadron was posted to Rangoon at the end of December (*David Armstrong*)

the inherent parallax of the two-piece system. Many pilots relied on the 'ring and post' sight instead. Later, the AVG's new P-40Es would have superior integrated optical gunsights.

The AVG's Tomahawks were armed with two synchronised 0.50-calibre guns in the upper cowling and two rifle-calibre guns in each wing. Armourers bore-sighted the guns to a range of 900 to 1000 ft (no one recalls for sure now), and actually fired-in the guns rather than simply eyeballing and calculating this. But the weapons presented a few problems. Wing guns were not installed by Curtiss. CAMCO therefore had to obtain these independently, and only enough Browning 0.30-calibre guns could be found to equip two squadrons. To make up the shortage, a number of 7.92 mm guns were obtained and installed in First Squadron aeroplanes. Their origin is uncertain.

The fuselage guns in the Tomahawk were the excellent 0.50-cal M2 Brownings. These were factory- installed by Curtiss, as foreign buyers had no equivalent weapon they preferred. Fortunately, ammunition for all these guns was available from British supply dumps in Mandalay, Bahmo and elsewhere. Chuck Baisden recalls that the wrong ammunition was loaded in wing guns a few times when aircraft from different AVG squadrons operated together, but the errors were always caught because it was their practice to charge the wing guns on the ground prior to flight. Some 0.30-cal guns manufactured by the Hi-Standard Company proved to be of low quality and gave problems as well, but diligent servicing kept reliability problems to a minimum.

Baisden also recalls that the AVG had plenty of guns and ammunition for operations, and most of the ammunition was good. He did have hang-fire problems with some of the 0.50-cal incendiary ammunition at Kunming, however, so it was reserved for use in the wing guns of the P-40E Kittyhawks when they began to arrive.

Armorer Keith Christensen had no problems with any of the ammunition – the big problem was keeping the guns clean and rust-free in the tropical climate. Third Squadron Armorer Joe Poshefko recalls that the guns would rust in a day if not serviced. Christensen remembers that they used a lot of oil and grease to inhibit rust, and depended on the first round fired to clear out any residual corrosion in the barrel. He recalls that most of the AVG's machine gun ammunition was already belted, but they had to belt some themselves. Poshefko recalls that much of the ammunition he handled was not intended for aircraft guns. AVG armourers generally used a sequence of two armour piercing rounds, two ball rounds, and a tracer.

The AVG's fighters were also shipped without radios, so as the aeroplanes arrived in Toungoo the communications men removed the existing R/T wiring harness and installed an antenna, wiring and radio equipment obtained on the civilian market. This radio gear consisted of RCA 7-H transceivers, 'intended for Piper Cubs' according to Group Communications specialist Robert M Smith. Another Communications man, Rolland Richardson, estimates that during operations, one fighter in three had a properly working radio at any given time, and the range was very short and spotty in any event. On the other hand, the ground communications equipment used in the famous Chinese warning net, which consisted of 400-watt twin-channel radios, was excellent. Unfortunately, the AVG operated for months outside the limits of this system.

Most of the AVG's Tomahawks were equipped only with wide, khaki-coloured lap belts, probably because end-users installed their own shoulder harnesses. But a few aircraft can be seen in photos with visible harness straps. And a few – sometimes the same aeroplanes – also had rear-view mirrors. Why only some aeroplanes would have these items is unknown, although it is likely that these details were just two equipment variations in Tomahawk production in early 1941.

Since the AVG's Tomahawks were taken from production lines working on a British contract, it has been widely assumed that Curtiss painted them in exact matches of the Dark Earth, Dark Green and Sky colours in use on RAF fighters in 1940-41. In fact it is now clear that Curtiss – and other American manufacturers as well – were not so fastidious, and instead typically used paints from their current suppliers that were close matches for the colours specified by foreign customers. Most of these paints were likely based on current US military camouflage standards.

Curtiss employed DuPont enamel camouflage paints on its products in 1940-41, and this included the brown and green colours used on the pattern camouflage of the Tomahawks shipped to Burma. The Dark Earth brown colour (DuPont 71-065) appears to have been virtually identical to Army Air Corps colour Rust Brown 34, while DuPont Dark Green (DuPont 71-013) was virtually identical to Army Air Corps Dark Green 30. Whether they *were* those specific colours is uncertain, but they are certainly indistinguishable from them, and also 'close enough' to the green and brown in use by the Royal Air Force.

Curtiss employed other colours on its fighters, however, including a sandy earth brown colour (DuPont 71-009). This shade has no analogue in the pre-war American colour standards, but it is similar to British Light Earth, and was perhaps intended for use on Desert Air Force Tomahawks. Period colour photos suggest that this colour was used on a few of the AVG's Tomahawks instead of the darker brown. Second Squadron pilot Robert Layher recalls noticing that, when seen side by side, some AVG Tomahawks had more 'vivid' camouflage on top than others. But it is unlikely that many casual observers would have noticed any significant difference between the colours on Curtiss's products and those on aircraft painted more exactly to British standards. Even fewer would have cared.

The lower surface camouflage of the AVG's Tomahawks is even more interesting. While British contracting officers would likely have specified the complex greenish colour known as Sky at the time these aircraft were ordered, the best colour photographs and film of AVG Tomahawks indicate that their lower surfaces were in fact painted *light grey*. It appears that other American manufacturers also frequently used light grey rather than Sky, and in fact British manufacturers had themselves employed a range of light blues, greys and greens when first coming to grips with the new requirement for Sky undersurfaces in mid-1940.

As yet no clear explanation for this anomaly has been found. Perhaps American manufacturers simply misunderstood British requirements that often rendered the name as 'Sky Type S Grey.' Indeed the observed light grey is remarkably similar to British Sky Grey. Or perhaps the requirements of other customers, or evolving British specifications for tropical schemes, were a factor. In any event, another existing American military colour, Aircraft Grey (later designated ANA 512), is an excellent match for both British Sky Grey and the observed colour on the bottom of the AVG's Tomahawks. But there is one additional complication – a colour photo shot in May 1942 reveals what appears to be Neutral Grey on the rear lower fuselage of two AVG Tomahawks! Unfortunately, no other photographs have yet been found that shed further light on this.

The vast majority of the AVG's Tomahawks were finished in the same uppersurface camouflage pattern derived from the standard British pattern for single-seat fighters. But while British practice was to specify a 50-50 mix of regular and 'mirror image' ('A' and 'B') patterns, all but a handful of AVG Tomahawks were painted in one pattern. Curtiss workers used rubber mats when applying the paint, so the patterns were remarkably uniform and had sharp colour separations. The light grey was added last, with a straight, tight-sprayed edge with the topside colours.

Since Curtiss's export products were not actually fully assembled at the factory, they were painted in component form. As a result, the camouflage patterns seldom precisely matched up where the components were later joined together, such as at the wing roots and fins, and the rudders never had light grey on the bottom edge.

When the AVG's Tomahawks were uncrated at Mingaladon airfield, they were completely bereft of national markings of any kind. The masking mats used by Curtiss had the locations for insignia incorporated into the pattern so that they could be easily and consistently added upon final assembly. These were laid out according to British specifications. According to Pentecost, his men marked Chinese insignia on the first few aeroplanes that were assembled, but this practice was discontinued because of the time and effort required. It is also likely that the British opposed anything that raised the profile of this not-so-secret operation any more than absolutely necessary.

One old account mentions rumours of British pressure to remove the Chinese insignia after hostilities had commenced, and photos of a few aeroplanes assembled in the first weeks do show evidence of this. But two of the last aeroplanes assembled (number 99, delivered on 22 November, and number 92, delivered six days later) also had patches of an off-white colour on the undersides of their wings, although these were perhaps the result of repairs rather than markings changes.

RAF serial numbers were originally assigned to these Tomahawks as well, and so they may have been applied at the factory, then overpainted before shipment too. This is not apparent in photos, however. This may have been the case with RAF fin flashes as well.

The spinners were in the respective brown colour, although in photos weathering, touch-ups and leaking oil sometimes create the appearance of other colours. And contrary to some offhand remarks in wartime accounts, there is no reliable evidence that AVG personnel repainted spinners for decorative purposes, although of course anything could have happened once or twice. Film and photo evidence establish that most of the wheel covers were painted at the factory in either the light grey under-surface camouflage colour or the Dark Earth brown. A few were finished in Neutral Grey, however – no doubt a result of simultaneous production of export and Army machines, and the portability of these parts.

The AVG suffered from a severe shortage of tyres, and Tomahawks, with their high landing speed, wore them out quickly on rough airfields in the tropical heat. Within days this was an issue, so Crew Chief George Bailey and Line Chief Frank Van Timmeran fitted eight to ten aeroplanes with small sheet metal vanes on the wheel covers in order to induce wheel rotation before touch-down. In order to observe the effectiveness of this modification more easily, they painted the wheel covers of a few of these aeroplanes half-blue and half-orange.

Propeller blades were the usual black, with the tips marked in yellow according to prevailing US specifications. Many props can be seen in photos with no tip markings, though, probably a result of excessive weathering. The usual data stencils were placed near the root of the blades in white. Like all military aircraft, the AVG's Tomahawks were covered with small servicing and information markings, including, on the top of the cowling, a white rectangle with the word *PRESTONE* in black on it.

There were three fuel tanks in the Curtiss model H81-A-2 – two in the wing centre section, and the main fuel tank behind the pilot. The fuel filler caps for these tanks were respectively in the left wing root, and directly behind the cockpit on the left side, accessible through a cut-out in the rear Plexiglas. The filler for the oil tank was aft of the fuselage fuel filler cap. Immediately above the fuselage filler cap was stencilled *R.D.E./F/100*, probably in yellow. The two wing root fuel fillers were covered by small hinged doors, with black lettering (about one inch high) marking each location – the forward filler was marked *RESERVE FUEL*, and the aft filler door was marked *WING FUEL*. *R.D.E./F/100* was also stencilled between the two access doors, again probably in yellow.

A black *NO STEP* marking was also placed on each wing fillet. An identical marking was placed on the trailing edges of the wing, readable from the rear, about 18 inches out from the wing fillet. This lettering was executed in a style that can also be seen on P-40Es and Ks with two-colour camouflage schemes. In fact the factory camouflage and markings practices for P-40s of all types were remarkably similar. There were other servicing markings on these aircraft, such as vent, gun and drain labels, and labels at the tie-down points under the wing tips. However, there were no markings indicating the location of a first aid kit inside the rear fuselage access door.

Colour photos of newly-assembled Curtiss aircraft in the pre-Pearl Harbor time period indicate that yellow zinc chromate primer was used for protecting undercarriage doors, access panels and similar components. Wheel wells were protected with canvas liners painted the undersurface colour.

FORGING A PURSUIT GROUP

In the days before enough aeroplanes, pilots and equipment arrived at Kyadaw airfield to keep everyone busy, morale and conduct problems in the infant pursuit group grew alarmingly. As Group Personnel Clerk Ed Fobes recalled in something of an understatement for a television documentary, 'the gang were not all angels, far from it'. The absence of military discipline was no doubt a factor, and some of the men also found the primitive conditions and tropical climate at Toungoo unbearable.

In the afternoons the temperature climbed to almost 120 degrees in the shade, and the variety and size of insect, rodent and reptile pests was alarming. The barracks were rough, and the food was inedible, leading some men to a life-long fondness for ketchup. Some groundcrewmen also found that the pre-war military class system of 'officers and men' had not entirely disappeared from the attitudes of all the members of this volunteer 'civilian' organisation.

On 26 August eight pilots and one groundcrewman resigned and left. Third Squadron pilot Robert T Smith recorded in his diary that 11 pilots quit from September to mid-November. According to Robert Hotz's wartime book on the AVG, twelve pilots and six groundcrewmen resigned prior to 7 December 1941, and a further ten pilots and thirty-seven ground crewmen were 'dishonourably discharged' for all reasons after the beginning of hostilities. As Smith noted for television cameras a few years ago, the reaction of those who remained was 'good riddance. If they can't take it, why, let them go. And I guess that's the way Chennault thought of it'.

But most could cope with such conditions. Third Squadron Crew Chief Irving Stolet, who had spent several years riding the rails during the Depression, 'had been hungry before in America' and was used to 'roughing it'. But food would continue to be such a problem during operations at Rangoon that Crew Chief Carl Quick was converted to a cook even though he was needed badly on the flightline. And tropical diseases would also prove to be a serious problem. At one time or another virtually every AVG member was out of action with dysentery, malaria, dengue fever or other illnesses.

Third Squadron Crew Chief Frank Losonsky arrived at Kyedaw on 16 August 1941. At first he had to use automotive tools, but gradually specialist tools and equipment arrived. Initially, personnel and equipment were divided temporarily into A, B and C flights. Each flight would soon grow to squadron strength, with more definitive personnel and equipment assignments. The initial handful of aircraft was not assigned to squadrons, and ground personnel simply worked where they were needed. By mid-September the AVG's three squadrons were in place.

Third Squadron Crew Chief Edward Stiles recalls that the AVG was modelled on an Army Air Corps table of organisation that called for three squadrons of 18 aeroplanes each, with five or six in reserve, but of course this was never attained. In addition to squadron organisations, the group also had an Engineering Section that handled major rebuilding jobs at Toungoo and Kunming. A similar operation was located at the CAMCO

This snapshot of Second Squadron pilot Ed Rector perfectly illustrates the limited nature of the facilities available for Group Engineering at Toungoo in 1941-42. Nevertheless, it had rebuilt more than half a dozen wrecked aeroplanes on site by January 1942. Hill, Rector and Christman were inseparable friends, and possibly an inspiration for Christman's 'Three Aces' comics (*David Armstrong*)

plant at Loiwing. By 6 October there were 55 aeroplanes in service, with nine flown that day – the most up to that point. But many aeroplanes would not have all the necessary equipment installed until well into November.

AVG groundcrews were woefully under-strength by the standards of the day. The table of organisation for a 1941 Army Air Corps pursuit group called for a ground echelon of more than 1000 men, but the AVG signed up a total of only 186 ground personnel in all specialities.

Second Squadron Crew Chief George Bailey recalls that when combat operations started there were 51 crew chiefs for all three squadrons, and in practice each was responsible for two or three aeroplanes. Each radioman was responsible for five or six aeroplanes, and the armourers had to service no fewer than three aeroplanes at any given time. While the AVG Third Squadron had only five armourers, a typical USAAC squadron would have had twenty. But, unlike the regular military, there was no need for KP, guard duty, or other such details. And of course Chinese (and initially some Burmese) labourers provided invaluable help transporting ammunition and fuel, cleaning guns, doing sheet metal repairs, painting, vehicle driving and other such jobs.

A number of the group's former Army crew chiefs had prior experience with Tomahawks and Allison engines, and they were especially valuable in the primitive operating environment facing the AVG. Early operations, including a fatal crash, revealed chronic problems with the Curtiss fighter's thrust bearing lubrication. Third Squadron crew chiefs Leo Schramm and John Fauth, after talking with Allison representative Walt Pentecost, devised a solution.

A small 'dam' was fabricated behind the thrust bearing and a tube was run from the well-lubricated propeller governor back to the thrust bearing so that scavenged oil would spray onto it. Schramm's aeroplane (number 92), and perhaps a few others, received this modification and had no problems with thrust bearings. Schramm also rigged his aeroplane with a recalibrated tachometer that 'fooled' the engine governor and allowed an additional 200 RPM for take-offs.

The group's many training accidents spurred further creativity with the Tomahawk's technical orders. The Tomahawk of course sat on its tail on the ground, and this meant that the rudder was ineffective for ground handling. Fauth and Schramm reasoned that changing the ground stance of the aeroplane would marginally increase rudder control for landing and take off. The landing gear were of an oil-air type, so air was pumped into the tail oleo strut, raising it to almost full extension and lifting the tail by a few inches. They then reduced the air pressure in the main landing gear oleo struts, lowering the nose a fraction of an inch.

This wasn't all. Schramm and Fauth next increased the amount of 'droop' of the ailerons from about 3/8ths inch to about 5/8ths inch. This provided a little more lift at the wingtips, enhancing controllability. Third Squadron Engineering Officer Robert Brouk tested each of these changes, and unknowing pilots remarked on the improved handling of such modified aeroplanes. However, Schramm and Fauth had a hard time getting approval from Squadron Line Chief Glen Blaylock, who was more familiar with oil derricks than Tomahawks. But after he was replaced by Frank Van Timmeran nearly all Third Squadron aeroplanes

Charles R Bond's assigned Tomahawk number '5' (probably P-8198) is refuelled at Kyadaw in October-November 1941. Note the distinctive style of the identification numbers. This identification system was typical of Nationalist Chinese aircraft during this period, and a necessity as the inventory of fighters grew (Charles R Bond, Jr)

got these enhancements. 'Improving' on the technical orders for aircraft would not have been allowed in regular military units at that time.

Regular maintenance schedules were followed at Toungoo, and for as long as possible after the outbreak of hostilities. The most serious problem was the lack of spares – particularly propellers and propeller control units, tyres, solenoids and spark plugs. A few loads of spare parts were on their way to Burma in December 1941 but never arrived. At one point several CAMCO personnel resorted to scouring the Far East for spare tyres and spark plugs, but they enjoyed little success. Fortunately, adequate supplies of ammunition, fuel, oil and radiator coolant were available from British and Nationalist Chinese stocks. Two Pan-Am Airlines C-53s also brought some spare propellers and other parts to Loiwing on 14 April 1942, but it is unknown how much of this materiel could be put to use before the Japanese captured the airfield a few weeks later.

MARKINGS

The first markings on the aeroplanes were simply a Chinese Air Force serial number stencilled on the fin in small (about three-inch) white figures – P-8101, for example. These serials were assigned in an order corresponding to the Curtiss construction/serial number sequence, and not the order in which the aeroplanes were assembled.

Of course these could not be seen well at a distance, and so some AVG personnel hastily painted or chalked larger versions of the distinct last two digits on the fins or rudders of a few aeroplanes. Examples include the large '90' seen on P-8190 as it was ferried to Toungoo on 4 September and the large '15' seen on both sides of the rudder of P-8115. By mid-September squadron assignments were being made, and Tomahawk P-8115 also had '3d' hastily marked on its rudder.

As the number of aircraft and personnel grew, a rapid identification system consisting of large white numerals on the rear fuselage of the aeroplanes was put in place by Group Headquarters. Number block 1-33 was assigned to the First Squadron, 34-67 to the Second and 68-99 to the Third. These numbers began to appear on the aeroplanes as early as 29 August. Photos reflect that it took several weeks before the majority of fighters had received this treatment, however.

Any correlation between these 'side numbers' and the serials on the fin was only coincidental, unlike the informal recognition numbers mentioned previously. They consisted of large (about 21- to 24-inch) white numerals, with smaller numbers (about five- to six-inch) on the nose of most aeroplanes as well. They were probably painted at the squadron level, and several different styles can be seen in photographs.

There was a little initial confusion about the exact size and placement of these numbers, with a few aircraft having them first painted under the cockpit rather than on the rear of the fuselage. These were covered with dark green paint (probably within a matter of days), and properly sized numbers were added in the customary rear fuselage location. Photos also reveal that the side number of a few aircraft were a dirty white or light grey colour – either a function of grime or a deliberate attempt to improve ground concealment.

The matter of serial and tactical numbers of particular airframes is a surprisingly difficult subject. Because of the almost five-month assembly and testing period, and training and combat losses, there were never more than about 60 Tomahawks in service at any one time, and so not all fuselage numbers could have been used at once. In fact, it is quite likely that several available numbers were never used at all, and there are a few instances of fuselage numbers being associated with several different serials as airframes were rebuilt and components swapped.

Significant airframe rebuilding work started in November at Toungoo as training losses mounted. By the end of January 1942, some six or seven Tomahawks had been rebuilt from various cannibalised parts, and this process continued thereafter. As Crew Chief Frank Losonsky points out, it was highly unlikely for a fuselage number on a aeroplane to be changed when repair work was done, and when parts were swapped the crews did not disturb whatever markings were on them. Crew Chief George Bailey recalls one exception to this, however – the Second Squadron repainted its existing fuselage numbers just prior to deployment to Rangoon near the end of December in order to maintain an uninterrupted sequence.

Assignment of aircraft to pilots was done at the squadron level. First Squadron pilot Richard Rossi recalls that only about half the available aeroplanes were assigned to pilots, and each of these was assigned to only one pilot at a time. Assigning aeroplanes was one of Robert T Smith's jobs as Assistant Operations Officer for the Third Squadron. He selected

Former PBY pilot Edwin Conant – who was born John Perry but washed out of Army flight school and changed his name to get into Navy flight school – arrived at Toungoo on 29 October 1941. By 5 November he had wrecked three aeroplanes trying to land them like flying boats. Tomahawk '74' was the first casualty, on 31 October. The others were numbers '78' and '81' – they all flew again after repairs by Group Engineering. Conant stayed in the AVG until the end, but did not fly a combat mission until 24 May 1942. Note the overpainted number beneath the cockpit *(Frank Losonsky)*

number 77 for himself, both for good luck and because it was the jersey number of football legend 'Red' Grange.

Assignment of an aeroplane simply meant that the particular pilot would have first option to fly 'his' aeroplane on his duty days, if it was available. If not, he flew any other available aeroplane. On a pilot's days off, his assigned aeroplane, if serviceable, would be used by other pilots. Second Squadron pilot Robert Keeton's log book illustrates this – he flew 100 sorties in 23 different Tomahawks, 67 flights in 11 different Kittyhawks, and 14 trips in three other types. Of the Tomahawks, he flew his assigned aeroplane, P-8120, 20 times.

Third Squadron Flight Leader Robert T Smith was an Army Air Corps flight instructor at Randolph Field, and had never flown a Tomahawk until he joined the AVG. This January 1942 photo of Smith in the cockpit of his assigned Tomahawk '77' provides a view of some details not easily seen in most photographs, including the windscreen bracing, armour glass, grab handle and gunsight reflector installation. Note the two heavy vertical seams in the windscreen Plexiglas, often misinterpreted as metal framing.
(*R T Smith via Brad Smith*)

FLYING THE TOMAHAWK

And what was the Tomahawk like to fly? Robert T Smith, a former Air Corps flight instructor, took his first flight in one two days after arriving in Burma on 15 September 1941. He wrote years later that after gaining some altitude he;

'. . . was grinning and chuckling to myself like a kid with a beautiful new toy, and feeling terribly self-satisfied . . . I climbed on up to about 8000 ft while making a series of turns. The controls were not quite as sensitive as I'd expected, in fact they felt very much like those of the BT-9. I spent the next few minutes doing both power-on and power-off stalls, found plenty of warning in either case before the full stall occurred, and that recovery was swift and easy when the nose was dropped and power re-applied.

'I did a couple of three-turn spins, and again the recovery procedure and response was much like the BT-9. And finally, of course, I began to really wring the old girl out – the stuff I'd been itching to do for all these weeks; slow-rolls, snap-rolls, loops and Immelmanns, so much easier and so much more fun with all that power up front. About the only real surprise, however, was the tremendous speed that could be picked up in a dive in a matter of mere seconds – this thing dove like the proverbial streamlined brick, a characteristic for which all of us were to be extremely thankful in future months.'

Not surprisingly, opinions of the Tomahawk varied in relation to a pilot's prior experience. Second Squadron pilot Tex Hill, who later flew Mustangs, thinks that the Tomahawk was 'kind of a doggy aeroplane,' being heavy and not very nimble. On the other hand, it was an excellent weapons platform, and its firepower and speed were good. Just as important, its sturdiness made it perfect for the difficult conditions that faced the AVG.

Third Squadron pilot Ken Jernstedt had qualified in the F4F Wildcat while a Marine pilot. He thought the Tomahawk performed very well and had no real vices, particularly as he got more experience with it. In his opinion it was easier to land and handle on the ground than the Wildcat because its landing gear were more widely spaced and its low wing design provided a better centre of gravity. The fast diving speed of the Tomahawk also presented few problems for him because of his prior experience. Jernstedt feels that the firepower of the Tomahawk was also superior to the four wing guns of the early Wildcat.

Robert 'Buster' Keeton of the Second Squadron, who had come from a Navy flying boat squadron, says he liked the Curtiss fighter once he got used to it. He recalls no serious controllability problems, although his first

DAVID LEE 'TEX' HILL

David Lee 'Tex' Hill encountered the Tomahawk for the first time at Kyadaw. This photo (right) was taken at Mingaladon Airfield, probably on 29 January 1942. Born in Korea of missionary parents, Hill was flying SB2U dive-bombers from the *Ranger* on 'neutrality patrols' with VS-41 when he signed up for the AVG in March 1941. He was kept busy leading missions at Rangoon, and recalls that unlike many of the other pilots, he spent the nights 'in the boondocks' near the aeroplanes on the dispersal fields, rather than 'leading the life of Riley' with the British colonials.

He enjoyed his first success on a 3 January strafing attack on Raheng, when he was credited with shooting a Ki-27 'Nate' off James Howard's tail. He was hit by 33 rounds himself, however. After four more victories, he returned to Kunming in February and, between bouts of dysentery and malaria, assisted with testing bombing equipment and methods and ferrying aircraft from India. Following Jack Newkirk's death on 24 March, Chennault promoted him to command of the Second Squadron. He flew many of the risky 'morale missions' in March-April 1942, scoring three more aerial victories, and opposed what Chennault later called the 'pilot's revolt' of 18 April. He led missions against Japanese ground forces at the Salween River Gorge in May, and ended his AVG service with a victory tally of 11.25 recognised by CAMCO.

He agreed to extend his AVG contract for two weeks, then accepted a commission in the Army Air Forces in China as the first Commanding Officer of the 75th FS. He returned to the US in November 1942, but went back to China a year later as Commanding Officer of the 23rd FG – a position he held until October 1944. While there he was credited with the destruction of five more Japanese aircraft. (*Photo Copyright George Rodger*)

reaction, recorded in his diary, was that he did 'not like the way it handles in the air at all' because every change in speed required trim tab adjustments. At first he also 'hate[d] the way they pick up speed in a dive, altogether different than anything I have ever flown before'. Charles Mott wrote that the Tomahawk 'has no undesirable flying characteristics, lands nicely and handles well on the roll. The rate of climb is about 2400 ft per minute. It is a bit stiff on the controls, however, and does not seem to be as manoeuvrable as it might be. The cockpit is hot as hell'.

Robert Layher, another flying boat pilot, loved the Curtiss machine once he had learned where everything was, although he had never previously flown a fighter so did not have anything to compare it to. He thought the aeroplane had good responsive controls and a good roll rate, but without a multi-stage supercharger its performance was not good above 20,000 ft. He did not have many problems landing the aeroplane because he brought it in 'hot', on the wheels.

The long nose of the Tomahawk made a three-point landing risky, especially with the short airfield at Toungoo. Layher recalls that only three or four pilots had serious problems learning to operate the fighter, and not all of them were former flying boat pilots. Peter Wright of the Second Squadron, a former SB2U Vindicator pilot, thought the Tomahawk had no more vices than any other aeroplane, but these were compounded by the short and narrow landing strip at Toungoo.

Seen here at Wu Chia Ba airfield, Kunming, in mid-January 1942, Third Squadron Flight Leaders and former Marines Charles Older, Ken Jernstedt and Tom Haywood were also new to the ways of the Tomahawk. Older participated in the 23 and 25 December battles around Rangoon, where he assisted in the destruction of four Ki-21 'Sallys' and one Ki-43 'Oscar'. On 17 January 1942 he shared credit for two more Ki-21 bombers, and duly became the first official ace of the group. His final official score in the AVG was 10.08, and after disbandment he joined the USAAF. Older returned to China in 1944 and became Operations Officer and Deputy Commander of the 23rd FG, scoring an additional eight victories. After the war he began a legal career in California, where he is remembered as the presiding judge in the Charles Manson murder trial of 1970-71. In the centre distance of this picture can be seen the unnumbered 'photo ship' with its gaping shark mouth. (R.T. Smith via Brad Smith)

First Squadron pilot Charles Bond soloed on the Tomahawk on 18 November 1941, and wrote in his diary that;

'. . . I was eager to try acrobatics during my first flight. Slow rolls, loops, and Immelmanns were smooth after a few tries. The one characteristic of the aeroplane which is new to me is the sharp increase of rudder-pedal

ROBERT LAYHER

Second Squadron pilot Robert Layher also had no prior experience with the Tomahawk, having flown Catalinas with VP-12 in San Diego prior to joining the AVG. This photo (right) was taken by George Rodger at Mingaladon airfield on 29 January 1942. The AVG recruiter initially refused to even talk to Layher, but a dinner and bottle of Scotch solved the problem. He went with the Second Squadron to Rangoon at the end of December, and took part in the 19 January raid on Mae Sot, sharing in the destruction of a Japanese light bomber.

On 5 March he had a narrow escape from death while doing an underspeed roll over the Kunming airfield during an airshow for Generalissimo and Madame Chiang Kai-shek. Later that day the escort flight he was part of became lost, and they all had to belly in when out of fuel. Layher landed some

distance from the others. He was not wearing his flight suit with his 'blood chit' and was held by suspicious locals until they finally got the word that he was on their side.

Layher's next adventure was in leading five Chinese pilots ferrying some P-43 Lancers from India. After a series of fatal accidents and resignations, Layher ended up alone at Assam, India, with a Kittyhawk and two Lancers! Caleb Hayes, CO of a squadron of C-47s engaged in flying supplies over the 'Hump,' had no fighter escorts and was anxious about Japanese fighter activity in Burma. So Layher flew reconnaissance missions for several weeks with Hayes' deputy, Robert Scott, accompanying him in one of the Lancers. Layher stayed on for two extra weeks in China after the AVG disbanded, and was credited with .83 victories by CAMCO (*Photo Copyright George Rodger*)

pressure required to offset an extreme yaw to the left, particularly in high-speed dives. At 400 mph in a vertical dive it is almost impossible to hold enough left rudder to correct for the drastic yaw without maximum rudder trim.'

Bond recalled that his first landing was good because he came in 'wheels first with tail up'. He had been warned that the aeroplane had a tendency to ground loop. Bond also flew a 'high altitude indoctrination flight' on 2 December, and found

that 23,000 ft was 'just about . . . maximum ceiling' for his Tomahawk. Altitude performance was perhaps the most serious fault of the entire P-40 series, as the aeroplane was originally conceived as a low altitude aircraft. AVG pilot Erik Shilling is effusive in his praise of the P-40 series, and he maintains that the service ceiling of the AVG's Hawks was over 30,000 ft, but he is probably recalling experiments he made with crewmen Charlie Engle and Henry Olson that improved fuel pressurisation at higher altitudes.

But getting the AVG fully operational proved to be more difficult than had been anticipated. By early November about ten aeroplanes had been wrecked in accidents, and another ten or so were unserviceable. The accidents then increased as more of the less-experienced pilots arrived and began to check out on the Tomahawk. Robert T Smith remarked a few years ago that 'we lost a lot of aeroplanes (in accidents). At one time I think Chennault was about fit to be tied, figuring my God, if we keep going like this another six weeks, we won't have any aeroplanes left to fight with'.

There were 52 separate training accidents before Christmas day, with seven on 3 November, or 'circus day', alone. By the time the AVG deployed for action 45 aeroplanes had been wrecked or were unservice-able at one time or another due to a lack of replacement parts. According to one source at least eight Second Squadron aeroplanes were wrecked in accidents before hostilities commenced. Groundcrews struggled to cannibalise wrecks to make flyable aeroplanes, and of course the increasing number of accidents created more available 'parts' for this purpose.

On 2 December there were 78 aircraft at Toungoo, but only 62 were in commission – 68 had radios, and 60 were fully armed. When war began five days later, there were only 54 serviceable aircraft available.

CHENNAULT'S 'KINDERGARTEN'

With such a disparate assemblage of pilots, extensive training was obviously essential if the group was to have any success. Chennault thus instituted what Charles Bond referred to as his 'kindergarten'. This was to consist of 50 hours each of ground school and flight training. Chennault's legendary lectures started each training day at six or seven in the morning, followed by flight training. This consisted of type familiarisation, formations, basic tactics and air-to-air mock combats. In November

First Squadron Flight Leader Charles R Bond was also a Tomahawk novice, having been an Army Air Corps Ferry Command pilot when he heard about the AVG. Here, he is seen preparing to take off in Edward J Liebolt's assigned aeroplane. Note the improvised gun sight reflector bracket, the rear view mirror and the faintly visible fuel stencilling. Bond only arrived in Burma on 12 November 1941, but within days was instrumental in creating the insignia for both the AVG and the First Squadron. First Squadron Flight Leader Ed Liebolt, a former Army pilot, went missing in action on 25 February 1942 near Rangoon. His fate remains a mystery (*Charles R Bond, Jr*)

some ground target gunnery was added. There was no aerial gunnery practice at all, however, and this was the greatest shortcoming of the programme. As Peter Wright notes, Chennault was a 'born teacher'. Charles Bond wrote that;

'Chennault taught everything he knew about fighting the Japanese. He emphasised that their pilots fought by the book, then he handed out Japanese flying and tactics manuals that had been captured and translated into English. He said that enemy pilots were brave fighters with plenty of guts, but that they lacked initiative and judgement. They went into battle with a set plan and followed it no matter what happened. Bombers always held their formations, and fighters always tried the same tricks, regardless of the combat situation.

'Chennault extolled the virtues and advantages of the P-40 over the Japanese Zero. Particularly, he stressed our superior diving capabilities as compared to the Zeroes. He emphasised that over and over, and told us never, never try to dogfight with a Zero, particularly in turning combat. Hit and run! Hit and run, dive, and then come back to altitude. Of course always try to stay in groups of at least two. As soon as you find yourself alone, search the skies to rejoin someone.'

Robert T Smith noted that Chennault lectured the pilots with drawings and photos of the aeroplanes they would encounter, and indicated the best methods of attacking Japanese bombers. This invariably involved avoiding low speed turning engagements and using hit and run tactics to take advantage of the speed, firepower and ruggedness of their aircraft. He noted, however, that '. . . as time went on, some of us did engage in actual dogfights' on the rare occasion when they fought a single opponent.

Smith also remembered that Chennault's theory of flying in pairs simply didn't work in practice because AVG forces were almost always heavily outnumbered, and as soon as combat started it was 'every man for himself'. He observed that 'it would have taken not only a lot of will power but one hell of a pilot to stick on my wing once the action started'.

'Tex' Hill recalls that because he arrived in Burma fairly early (15 September 1941), his training consisted of the full 50 hours of lecture time and 50 hours of flight time. The most important lesson he recalls learning from Chennault was the importance of the two-aeroplane element and flights of four, in contrast to the three-aeroplane formation he had been taught in the Navy.

AVG pilots were trained to attack bombers in three elements. First was an 'A' (assault) element to start the attack and draw away any escorting fighters. The second, or 'B' (support) element would follow up against the now uncovered bombers, and a 'C' (reserve) element would provide high cover and support where most needed. Indeed, Chennault appears to have envisioned deploying his three-squadron group in the same way.

Hill also recalls that Chennault taught AVG pilots that the Japanese were very regimented in their plans and tactics, executing them like clockwork if not disrupted, but he cautioned that the individual aeroplane-handling of Japanese pilots was very good.

Kenneth Jernstedt arrived in Burma on 10 October, when training was already underway. It took a few days before he checked out on the Tomahawk, but he was able to participate in most of the training organised by Chennault. He recalls especially that Chennault described how to take advantage of the speed advantage of the Tomahawk. He also warned the pilots that they could not turn with the Japanese fighters, so they had to dive out and use superior speed to escape. He also told them that they would be outnumbered, so they must fly and fight with the idea of living to fight another day.

But some AVG pilots arrived in Burma too late to be fully trained when the war started, and a number of these had been signed up under the more 'flexible' recruiting standards. Robert Layher and Robert Keeton did not arrive until 12 November, and thus missed Chennault's training programme. Neither had flown single-engine aeroplanes in service, and they both had to transition with the BT-14 trainers available at Toungoo and learn 'on the job'. Keeton did not fly his first of four transition flights in the trainer until 1 December, and when the Second Squadron was deployed for action he was ordered to stay behind in Toungoo and help Ed Goyette test repaired aeroplanes.

In early February 1942 the field began to come under air attack, and during a test flight of Tomahawk P-8131 he encountered and shot down his first enemy aircraft. Notwithstanding this, he was still flying training and support missions well into March. Richard Rossi of the First Squadron also also arrived in Burma on 12 November. He learned from the other pilots 'on the job'. It was some time before he was able to even sit in one of the Tomahawks, and he had only one gunnery flight before he flew a combat mission, and that involved shooting at ground targets. The next time he fired his guns was at the enemy.

As of 2 December, AVG pilots had flown a total of 3293 hours in training. Those who had arrived earliest had completed an average of 40 hours each of classroom and flight training.

When the AVG was sent into action in December 1941 some 20 to 25 pilots had not yet completed the planned training course, including six in what Chennault then considered the best-prepared squadron, the Third. Weeks later many of these pilots were still not ready for combat operations as far as Chennault was concerned.

Japanese diplomatic officials in the United States had been aware that something unusual was going on as early as June 1941, and AVG veterans recall hearing broadcasts threatening to sink their ships before they could get to Asia. Japanese spies and consular personnel in Burma noted the August arrival of the first large contingent of AVG personnel there, and the likely hostile intentions of these American 'civilians' was remarked upon in a Japanese high-level military planning session in September. The Japanese flew a reconnaissance flight over Kyedaw on 18 October, and 48 hours later the AVG instituted alerts and patrols, although there were only 12 aeroplanes fully armed and ready for combat by then.

On 24 October Squadron Leaders Robert Sandell (First), John Newkirk (Second) and Arvid Olson (Third) scouted into Thailand for signs of a Japanese build-up, but found nothing. Another Japanese reconnaissance flight flew over Kyedaw on 26 October, and the AVG made a fruitless effort to intercept it. Erik Shilling and others attempted another unsuccessful interception of a Japanese intruder two days later. Further Japanese reconnaissance missions appeared in November, and AVG pilots conducted another scouting mission of their own but failed to find any evidence of Japanese units.

WARPAINT AND PIN-UPS

As the AVG neared operational status in November 1941, the matter of aircraft markings was added to all the other preparations under way. Nationalist Chinese insignia were painted on in the four wing positions as was the practice at the time. There were exceptions, however, and at least two aircraft (number '23' and an unidentified Third Squadron aeroplane) had no insignia on the wing undersurfaces, at least at the time they were photographed with all other markings in place.

The insignia were about 36 inches in diameter, although a few aeroplanes (mostly in the Second Squadron) can be seen with slightly larger insignia on the wing undersides. They were probably painted by Chinese workers, undoubtedly with blue and white paints and stencils obtained from Nationalist Chinese Air Force sources. The insignia were placed outboard of the standard RAF positions, and clear of both the leading edge and the ailerons. The colour used for this (and for other blue AVG markings) was a medium or royal blue – at the time the Nationalist Chinese standard. This paint rapidly faded to a much lighter shade, however, particularly on the tops of the wings.

Squadron identification bands were also among the first items to be painted. These were five or six inches in width, and placed just forward of the tail group. Each squadron had its own identification colour: white for the First, blue for the Second and red for the Third.

The names of assigned pilots were also painted on some of the aircraft in mid November too, although some may have been added earlier. Like other AVG-specific markings, there was no official policy or directive on this. Peter Wright recalls that such markings were not placed on Second Squadron aeroplanes, and not all First and Third Squadron aeroplanes had them either. Where they did appear they were painted in small (about two-inch) white letters, typically on the port side just in front of the cockpit. There were several variations in lettering styles and sizes.

Crew chiefs were sometimes also identified. Several aeroplanes featured the name of the crew chief in small letters on the fin (for example 'Curran' on aeroplane number '33'). First Squadron Crew Chief Frank Andersen (Jacobson during his service in the AVG) also recalls painting 'Jake' on the fins of

Both pilot Charles Bond and Crew Chief Walter J Dolan of Rochester, New York, were identified on 'their' Tomahawk '5'. Note the *PRESTONE* stencil and the Chinese insignia on the starboard wing (*Charles R Bond, Jr*)

27

the aeroplanes he crewed. Third Squadron Crew Chief Stan Regis had his name inscribed on the starboard side of aeroplane number '75' opposite the pilot inscription.

The Third Squadron had decided on a 'Hell's Angels' theme for its own markings some weeks before national insignia began to be marked in November. Third Squadron pilot Ken Jernstedt recalls that the squadron mascot had already been agreed upon when he arrived in Burma on 10 October 1941. No one now remembers who originated the idea, but veterans agree that the inspiration was the 1930 motion picture of the same name, re-released in 1940.

Photographs reveal that the first 'Hell's Angel' figure was painted, probably with white water paint, on the rear fuselage of Tomahawk P-8115 (later number '69') during September 1941, perhaps by pilot Fred Hodges. This was subsequently removed, and Crew Chief Stan Regis devised the actual 'Hell's Angel' figures seen on Third Squadron aeroplanes. These were in red and white, and placed on both sides of the fuselage between the cockpit and the exhaust stacks. Regis told Frank Losonsky that he got his inspiration 'from a pin-up picture', almost certainly referring to the artwork of George Petty in *Esquire* magazine.

Regis was almost certainly the first in the AVG to begin painting such insignia, and thus also the first American of the war to emblazon such pin-up inspired 'nose art' on a combat aircraft. Losonsky recalls that although Regis created some patterns, or templates, to facilitate the process, much of the work was done freehand. No two angels were posed in exactly the same way – even the two on either side of the same aircraft – although of course there are only so many poses the human body can make, even where 'realism' is rather idealised!

Each insignia was about two feet in height, and took about a half-hour to paint. Losonsky also recalls that sometimes the red part was painted first, and sometimes the white part, and since this decorative work was frequently interrupted for other more important business, one often saw incomplete markings on aeroplanes. It appears that Regis did most of the work at first, but Losonsky recalls that there were many angels that were actually painted by Chinese helpers. Perhaps that is where the templates came into play, and this is also suggested by close examination of photos. Considering that some of these markings were still being added to

Third Squadron Crew Chief Stanley Regis shows off one of his 'Hell's Angels' squadron insignia. The Third Squadron agreed on its mascot several weeks before the others. After serving with the AVG, Regis joined China National Airways Corporation with fellow Crew Chief Frank Losonsky, then Hindustan Aircraft at Bangalore, India. They eventually returned to the United States and got civilian jobs in the USAAF maintenance division at Clark Field, in the Philippines. While there, they also started an import/export company that specialised in war surplus material, then met Col Pappy Gunn, who was starting Philippine Airlines in Manila. They helped him assemble a technical staff for the airline, and continued working for him while still running the import/export business. Regis then returned to the USA to run the operation at that end, but things did not go as well as planned and he took a job with War Assets in America. After that, he got a job with Bendix International and finally settled in South Africa, running a tree farm. He passed away about four years ago (*Frank Losonsky*)

Robert T Smith poses for the camera in Tomahawk '77' at Kunming in January 1942. Smith flew this machine in the famous Rangoon battles on 23 and 25 December 1941. On Christmas Day, his fighter was hit 34 times by 7.7 mm rounds (several of which penetrated the cockpit) and debris from exploding bombers. Smith in turn claimed a Ki-43 'Oscar' and two Ki-21 'Sallys' destroyed (*R T Smith*)

KENNETH JERNSTEDT

Kenneth Jernstedt (right) is seen sat in his assigned Tomahawk '88' (P-8121) at Kunming in early 1942. He flew his first combat mission at Rangoon on 23 December, and was credited with the destruction of one Ki-21. Two days later he downed a Ki-27. His next saw action when he was sent to Magwe, which was then under heavy aerial attack.

On 18 March Jernstedt and Bill Reed conducted a surprise attack on the Japanese airfields at Mudon and Moulmein. Using Chuck Baisden's improvised incendiary and grenade delivery systems, they were credited with the destruction of 15 enemy aircraft on the ground – the most ever by two AVG pilots in one mission. On 22 March, while intercepting a large Japanese attack on Magwe with four other

AVG Tomahawks and six RAF Hurricanes, he was hit through the canopy and wounded by glass fragments. He successfully landed and was evacuated to Kunming for treatment. Jernstedt later claimed the destruction of two of the bombers, but because he did not press the matter, and had not been able to file a timely combat report, they were not recognised by CAMCO. Tomahawk '88' was destroyed on the ground that same day. Jernstedt was credited with downing a Ki-43 during the 28 April battle with the 64th Sentai near Loiwing. After the AVG disbanded, he joined Republic Aviation as a test pilot, and after the war he returned to his native Oregon a nd became a State Senator. Jernstedt's official AVG tally is 10.5 kills. (*Photo Copyright Chuck Baisden*)

reallocated aeroplanes quite late in AVG service, this is not surprising. Regis painted these insignia on AVG flight jackets by himself, however.

Perhaps these Third Squadron embellishments inspired First and Second Squadron personnel to begin thinking of markings for their own units, but for whatever reason the creative process began in earnest in mid-November 1941. This would lead first to the 'shark's teeth' and then to the other squadron markings when shark heads were adopted for the entire group. As it turned out, however, there simply was not enough time for marking each and every aeroplane with all the possible group or squadron markings, and after combat operations started there were few opportunities to complete unfinished work.

Close-up view of the cockpit of Chuck Older's Tomahawk '68' (P-8109) in early 1942. The five victory flags had been replaced with ten smaller ones by May 1942 (*Chuck Baisden*)

Thus many First Squadron aeroplanes, and nearly all those of the Second Squadron, would wear no squadron insignia when combat began. A few aeroplanes would even lack 'shark's teeth'.

— SHARKS OF THE AIR —

First Squadron pilot Charles R Bond, Jr recalls that after dinner with some British civilians near Toungoo on 15 November 1941, he saw the 2 November issue of the *Illustrated Weekly of India*. On the cover was a striking colour photograph of some RAF Tomahawks with shark's teeth markings. Bond says that Erik Shilling and several other pilots were looking over his shoulder at the time. He exclaimed that he wanted to paint his aeroplane that way and everyone thought it was a good idea.

He got permission to take the magazine with him, and next morning pedalled his bike to the Toungoo train station, which had a shop selling various goods. He bought little cans of red, white, black and green 'oil paint' to 'jazz up the aeroplanes' and returned to the field. He then chalked the design on the aeroplane he had been flying and began painting. Unknown to him at the time, pilot Erik Shilling was doing the same on a different part of the field!

Shilling also recalled seeing that issue of the *Illustrated Weekly of India*, but he was impressed by a photo in it of some shark-toothed German Messerschmitt Bf 110s of ZG 76. He recalled in his 1993 memoir that he went to the airfield the next morning with pilots Lacy Mangleburg and Ken Merritt and chalked a shark head on an aeroplane he had been flying. He then painted it with the only paint he could find – white and blue from Chinese painters working on insignia, and red paint he got from Stan Regis, who was then painting his 'Hell's Angels' on Third Squadron aeroplanes.

At the time Shilling was doing engineering and photo-reconnaissance work for Group Headquarters while assigned to the Second Squadron. He recalled that he, Mangleburg and Merritt then went to Chennault and asked him if the shark head marking could be used as their squadron's insignia.

Bond recalls that while he was working on his shark head Chennault drove up in his Studebaker truck and had a look at it. Bond was a new arrival in the AVG at the time and didn't know Chennault yet, so they didn't say anything and Chennault drove off. Bond now surmises that after that Chennault told Shilling that the marking should be used for the group, not just his squadron, and from that point the idea spread rapidly.

First Squadron pilot Richard Rossi recalls that that issue of the *Illustrated Weekly of India* had arrived one Sunday at the Toungoo train station where many AVG members ate, and the next day it seemed that everyone had a copy. Considering that the issue also contained articles on 'Japan's Air Force' and 'Another China 'Back Door', it is easy to understand why it would get the attention of AVG members.

Third Squadron pilot Paul Greene recalls having a copy of it, and deciding that he could improve on the shark head design shown on the cover. Third Squadron Armorer Chuck Baisden remembers seeing the magazine too, and so does Second Squadron pilot Peter Wright.

Walter Pentecost, who wrote the first published account of this source of inspiration in the 1 August 1942 issue of *Liberty* magazine, said that he saw it while catching up on

On Sunday, 15 November 1941 Charles Bond saw a colour photograph of RAF No 112 Sqn Tomahawks with shark's teeth insignia on the cover of a recent issue of the *Illustrated Weekly of India*, and he decided that all First Squadron aeroplanes should be painted that way. One of the first aircraft to be decorated was Bond's own Tomahawk, number '5', seen here. Bond's design set the pattern for many of the shark heads on AVG fighters (*Charles R Bond, Jr*)

ERIK SHILLING

Then-Second Squadron pilot and Group Photo Officer Erik Shilling also saw the copy of the *Illustrated Weekly of India* on 15 November and set to work the next day on the 'photo-ship' he had been flying. His handiwork can be seen in this photo (right) taken by Clare Boothe Luce at Kunming on 11 April 1942 – the original appeared in colour in the 20 July 1942 edition of *Life* magazine. Shilling is sitting on the nose with First Squadron pilot William E Bartling to his left and Third Squadron pilot Frank W Adkins in the cockpit. On the wing are First Squadron pilot Joe Rosbert and Group Finance Officer and Second Squadron pilot George L 'Pappy' Paxton. Standing in front are First Squadron Flight Leaders Charles Bond and Robert Little. Note the lack of wing guns. Other photos reveal that in addition to Shilling's distinctive blue-lipped shark head, this machine had a 'swami head' insignia located just behind Rosbert and Paxton.

Shilling had been a pilot in the US Army Air Corps, serving in, among other organisations, the 23rd Composite Group, the First Pursuit Group, Base Engineering at Langley Field, and the 41st Long Range Reconnaissance Squadron. He arrived in Burma in August 1941 and was assigned to Group Operations and Training and Group Engineering, where he handled flight-testing, troubleshooting and accident investigations. He was considered one of the AVG's best pilots, and was chosen by Chennault to demonstrate the capabilities of the Tomahawk in a mock dogfight with an RAF Brewster Buffalo. The AVG's first mission after the outbreak of hostilities was Shilling's 10 December photo-reconnaissance flight to Don Muang airfield in Bangkok, Thailand, where Japanese aircraft were assembling for the Burma campaign. Later in December he led a disastrous ferry flight from Rangoon to Kunming. On 17 January 1942 he was part of a four-fighter flight that intercepted three unescorted 'Lily' bombers. All were downed, and he was credited with .75 of a kill, his total AVG score.

After the AVG he joined the China National Airways Corporation (CNAC) in India, and flew transports over the 'Hump' for the rest of the war, with breaks for service as a Republic test pilot and airline pilot for TWA. At the end of the war he joined Chennault's Chinese National Relief and Rehabilitation Air Transport, later renamed Civil Air Transport (CAT), which became a CIA-supported clandestine air force in support of the Nationalists during the Chinese civil war. After a short stint with the Indonesian Air Force he returned to CAT and participated in additional clandestine operations in Vietnam. In the mid-1950s he took a job as a pilot for Swissair, and retired from flying in 1960.
(*Photo Copyright Charles R Bond, Jr*)

his reading with pilot Raymond Hastey at the news-stand of the Strand Hotel in Rangoon.

Through the years various details of this story have been garbled, but everyone with an opinion on the matter, other than Shilling, has identified the Tomahawk cover photo as the model for the AVG's shark heads, and a look at photos confirms this influence. But the large gaping shark mouth painted by Shilling clearly has similarities with those of ZG 76's Bf 110s,

AVG shark heads were done applied freehand, using a chalk or pencil sketch. Here we see an incomplete paint job on Third Squadron Tomahawk '73' some time in late November or early December 1941. The nose number has been neatly blotted out. Note that Stan Regis' 'Hell's Angels' insignia was already complete when work on the shark head began (*Frank Losonsky*)

if only in retrospect. Chennault himself said that the AVG's shark heads 'copied the shark-tooth design [from] an RAF squadron in the Libyan Desert', although he mentions that the Germans had previously used such a design on their Messerschmitt 210s (sic).

Richard Rossi says that the shark head on Tomahawks 'just looked so good', and by the end of November all the aeroplanes that were not in maintenance had a shark head on them. Third Squadron Crew Chief Irving Stolet says he didn't really pay any attention to these things, but he does recall that it seemed like shark teeth just began to appear 'all of a sudden'.

Pilot Robert Keeton arrived in Toungoo on 12 November, and all he remembers is that a few days later shark's teeth started appearing on the aeroplanes. Robert Layher and Peter Wright both recall seeing the design on one aeroplane, and soon on many others 'pretty much at the same time'. Neither Layher nor Wright got involved with the artwork themselves, but Layher did notice two or three different people on the field working on shark teeth. Second Squadron Crew Chief George Tyrell says that at the time he didn't think such things were very important, and he noticed that the shark teeth 'just happened'.

Rossi, Layher and First Squadron Armorer Don Rodewald recall that before the shark idea was adopted, there had been some discussion of a dragon as a group motif, with the possibility of painting large dragons

Tomahawk '46', seen here with Second Squadron Flight Leader Robert Layher, was one of several Second Squadron aircraft that sported blue shark lips inspired by Shilling's work. This aeroplane was ultimately transferred to the Third Squadron, where its markings were repainted (*Robert Layher*)

down the side of each of the aeroplanes. Rossi says, however, that someone insisted, erroneously as it turned out, that the Nationalist Chinese opposed the use of old dynastic symbols for such things, and the idea got no further.

'Tex' Hill recalls that fellow Second Squadron pilot Bert Christman, (formerly a professional cartoonist, who would figure prominently in the artwork on the Second Squadron's aeroplanes), also sketched a possible group insignia or crest based on a 'flying tomahawk'

theme, but it was note adopted either. A wartime book states that Chennault had suggested a falcon too.

Armorer Chuck Baisden recalls that Stan Regis was involved with some of the shark heads, and that pilot Tom Haywood also took an interest in the work. He remembers that markings were generally handled by pilots and crew chiefs, with the men getting involved – or not – as they saw fit. Russell Whelan's wartime book states that most of the artwork was by Erik Shilling, Stan Regis, Bill McGarry and Bert Christman.

Pilot Paul Greene painted his own shark head, and recalls that it took him about a day to do. He recalls that red, white and black predominated in the design, and he thought his was one of the nicest ones done! Ken Jernstedt thinks that Stan Regis may have been involved in painting his aeroplane, number '88'. Armorers Keith Christensen and Joe Poshefko also recall seeing Stan Regis painting some shark heads. Frank Losonsky can't recall if Regis was involved with these or not, but he saw Chinese painters working on shark heads too.

George Bailey remembers that pilot Frank Schiel got some paint in Rangoon for this purpose because it was unavailable in Toungoo. He also recalls seeing Crew Chief Joe Peeden doing the painting on Ed Rector's aeroplane (number '36').

Losonsky says that as far as he knows, one person per squadron was probably designated to handle such things. But, as Chuck Baisden observed, it was a matter of interest and ability (and time). If a crew chief or pilot wasn't a good painter, or was just not interested, then they would have someone else do the job for them. Ken Jernstedt noticed that various groups of aeroplanes – probably those that were frequently lined up together on the flightline – often had similar styles to their shark heads because those crews worked more closely together.

Greene also notes that he and others collaborated to some extent, and that each shark head was the product of both collaboration and individual ability. In his opinion some weren't done so well, and the Third Squadron overall had the best ones. Jernstedt remembers that each squadron seemed to have its own style of shark head, with those of the Third Squadron being the most elaborate.

The painting process took time, since aircraft could not be spared from other activities. Robert T Smith worked on the paint job of his aeroplane

Stan Regis poses beneath his handiwork on Tomahawk '75' (P-8186) at Toungoo probably in early December 1941. Regis not only designed the Third Squadron's insignia, he probably supervised work on some of their shark heads as well. The Third Squadron had the most intricate shark head paint jobs in the AVG, with frequent use of accent stripes and other colourful embellishments. The shark head on this aeroplane was revised when the unit was ordered to Kunming at the beginning of 1942. Note the plain wheel covers and lack of underwing insignia on the fighter in the background (*Chuck Baisden*)

(number '77') between training flights and maintenance from 18 to 29 November. Charles Bond did not finish his assigned aeroplane (number '5') until 6 December, and he recalls helping with Ed Rector's aeroplane on 5 December. First Squadron pilot George Burgard was assigned Tomahawk '12' on November 30, and painted it from 2-4 December.

Pilot Joe Rosbert wrote that there was 'a flurry of activity' right after Pearl Harbor to finish the work. But it is clear that a few aircraft never received shark's teeth. No stencils or patterns were used for the shark heads. Losonsky recalls that they were first outlined on the aeroplanes in chalk, as Bond and Shilling described, then hand-painted. Paul Greene used either chalk or pencil to sketch his design.

The most common colour scheme, at least in the First and Second Squadrons, consisted of black lips, white teeth, a red tongue, and eyes in white and red. The camouflage paint showed inside the mouth area on most aircraft, and the small nose numbers were often painted out when the shark heads were added.

But with a number of men applying themselves to the task, there were many detail variations, and indeed, several stylistic 'schools' emerged. A few machines, particularly in the First Squadron, sported what can only be described as white dimples at the rear of the mouth. Some First Squadron shark heads also had more elaborate eyes. Erik Shilling recalls that after he painted his fighter 'we proceeded to do the same for Lacy's (Mangleburg) and Ken's (Merritt) aeroplane', and he also chalked some shark heads on other aeroplanes but left the painting to others. As a result of this influence, at least three other Second Squadron aeroplanes (number '36', '46' and '47') had blue used to outline the shark mouth in addition to Shilling's photo Tomahawk.

Photographs confirm that the shark head designs of many Third Squadron machines were more intricately detailed than those of the other two squadrons, and employed a wider range of colours. Perhaps this was the influence of the talented Stan Regis, or the result of that squadron's head start on the others. Surprisingly, at Toungoo in November the shark heads of many Third Squadron aeroplanes sported *brown* tongues edged

Line-up of Third Squadron aircraft at Toungoo on 9 December 1941 undergoing a final check before deployment to Mingaladon airfield (*Chuck Baisden*)

in red. This can be clearly seen in colour photos of aeroplanes number '75', '91' and '99', among others.

Perhaps red paint was in short supply at Toungoo, but the brown was repainted with red, and other detail changes were made, when the Third Squadron moved to Kunming in January 1942. Ken Jernstedt and Frank Losonsky both recall such changes being made by the Chinese painters, whom Losonsky remembers were real 'perfectionists'. In addition to freshening up the shark heads and Hell's Angel figures, they also added the famous red/white/blue pinwheels to the wheel covers of the Third Squadron's aeroplanes. These were 'handed' for left and right sides, but of course sometimes placed on the wrong wheels.

Another distinctive feature of many Third Squadron shark head markings was that the area inside the mouth was painted-in. A mixed light grey that closely matched the colour of the aircraft's lower surfaces was most common. Examples are Tomahawks '68', '75', '77' and '91'. A slightly darker shade of mixed grey was used on aeroplane number '69'. Tomahawk '92' had a medium blue-grey colour inside the shark mouth, while aeroplane number '71' appears to have had the area inside the mouth painted the Chinese insignia blue colour. It is likely that some of these colours were changed or added at Kunming in January.

There were other embellishments to Third Squadron shark head designs that can be seen both before and after the move to Kunming. Many had thin black striping on the edges of the teeth and/or tongue, such as sharks number '75' and '77'. Some, like number '77', also had red edging on the inside of the lips. This detail was added to aeroplane number '75' in Kunming. Still others had pink or orange edging on the inside of the lips and top of the tongue, such as Tomahawk number '68'.

The eyes of many shark heads in all three squadrons also varied from the simple white and red pattern. Some on First Squadron shark heads were quite elaborate, with eccentrically shaped pupils and intricate shading and detailing in various colours. Charles Bond's Tomahawk '5' is an example of this. Some painters used other colours for the eye's pupil, such as black on aeroplane number '57', or blue on Tomahawks '36' and '47'.

Other artists painted the pupils in two concentric colours, with black and red seen on aeroplanes number '7', '25' and '75'. Pupils of red and grey or pink can be seen in photos of aeroplanes number '49', '77' and '84'. The shark head on Tomahawk '33' had orange and brown pupils, while those on aeroplane '91' were light blue and black, and other combinations of the available colours must have existed too.

But as the weeks passed and wear and tear took their toll, nearly all AVG aeroplanes came to have simpler red, white and black shark head designs like those originally used for most of the aeroplanes of the First and Second Squadrons.

Third Squadron Flight Leader William Reed stands next to his assigned Tomahawk '75' at Toungoo on 9 December 1941. Note the residue of the chalk sketch, the unadorned wheel covers and nose numbers. The shark head would be revised weeks later in Kunming. Bill Reed was already flying P-40s with the Army Air Corps when he joined the AVG. He was involved in virtually all of the Third Squadron's major engagements, beginning with the battles over Rangoon on 23 and 25 December. Perhaps Reed's most famous exploit was the 18 March pre-dawn attack on Japanese bases at Mudon and Moulmein with Ken Jernstedt, where he was credited with the destruction of no less than eight enemy aircraft on the ground. He ended his service with the AVG with 10.5 air and ground kills to his credit. After the AVG, Reed rejoined the Army Air Forces. With the rank of major he commanded the 7th Fighter Squadron of the Chinese-American Composite Wing, and was credited with an additional seven aerial victories. In January 1944 he was killed while bailing out of his aircraft after returning from a mission in bad weather, being apparently knocked unconscious before he could open his parachute (*Chuck Baisden*)

These 'replacement' markings were typically applied less fastidiously than the originals, as the time and materials for such artistry disappeared.

THE FIRST PURSUIT, AND PANDA BEARS

Charles Bond recalls that Chennault's decision that the shark head should be a group marking 'ended the possibility that the teeth could be a squadron insignia, so everyone had to think up something different'. That started discussions, and Bond recalls that late one night he was in the bar with pilots Richard Rossi and Bob Prescott. Rossi quipped that the 'first pursuit' had to be Eve chasing Adam in the Garden of Eden. There was an uproar of laughter, and Bond thought it was 'a hell of a good idea'.

So next morning when he was working on the teeth on his aeroplane, he also chalked the outline of a Garden of Eden apple and 'toothpick' Adam and Eve figures on it. He painted the apple red and the stick figures white. He recalls that a week or so later he was talking to Chennault about some subject, and as he was leaving Chennault told him that the red apple 'ain't gonna do'. Bond asked why, and Chennault explained that 'it looks like the Japanese sun. Your buddies seeing you in combat might check you out as an enemy and shoot you down'. Bond thought, 'hell, there goes my idea,' but then on the way out it occurred to him that there are green apples too. He mentioned that to Chennault and got his approval. The apple was repainted light green, and that then became the basis for the insignia of the First Pursuit Squadron, the 'Adam and Eves'.

But one further detail remained – while talking over his creation with fellow pilot Jim Cross, Bond got the idea of adding a black snake to the design, and this addition then became the norm. Other artists also frequently added white lettering on or above the snake stating '1st Pursuit', 'First Pursuit', or '1st Pur'. The white 'toothpick' figures always faced the front of the aeroplane. The insignia were typically about 20-24 inches in diameter.

Richard Rossi recalls that there was a second version of the insignia that featured fully formed cartoon figures. Robert Neale's last Tomahawk, '7', is the only one with these cartoon figures that has so far been found in photographs, although Charles Bond recalls hearing that Flight Leader Robert Prescott's version of the insignia also had fully formed cartoon figures. Richard Rossi recalls that Cross's aeroplane (number '13') had 'one of each' style on it. Other small details varied from aeroplane to aeroplane, such as the grinning snake wearing a top hat on Robert Little's fighter (number '33'). First Squadron insignia were typically placed near the trailing edge of the wing, just forward of, or on, the baggage compartment door on the port side. But by the time this work got underway time was rapidly running out. Many First Squadron aeroplanes never received their insignia.

The Second Squadron took even longer to arrive at a mascot. No one

Jim Cross's assigned Tomahawk number '13' sports both Charles Bond's original chalk sketch for the 'First Pursuit' insignia and the finished item, complete with serpent (*Charles R Bond, Jr*)

now seems to remember how they became the 'Panda Bears', but wartime sources credit Squadron Leader John Newkirk with deciding upon this mascot after a long and loud argument among the pilots. As Second Squadron pilot James Howard noted in his memoir, no one seemed to like the 'Panda Bear' nickname very much.

Crew chief Frank Anderson recalls that at the time he thought the idea of a panda bear mascot 'stunk'. Peter Wright thinks that a quiet, peaceful teddy bear-like creature simply seemed out of place as a mascot for a fighter squadron. Second Squadron pilot Robert Layher believes that Bert Christman was one of the advocates for this mascot. In any event, no standard panda bear squadron insignia was actually painted on any of the aeroplanes. Wright agrees, and 'Tex' Hill notes that the well-known 'sitting' panda bear cartoon seen in some illustrations post-dated AVG service. Second Squadron Crew Chief George Bailey recalls being told that Disney Studios had created decals of this sitting panda bear for the AVG, but as far as he knows they never arrived in China.

Second Squadron pilots finally decided that rather than a uniform insignia, they would have Christman paint individual panda-based pilot caricatures on their aeroplanes. In doing so Christman became America's

BERT CHRISTMAN

Bert Christman, Ed Goyette and Ed Rector (right) are seen sight-seeing on the road to Mandalay, during the Autumn of 1941. Goyette later headed the Engineering Detachment at Kyadaw during the Rangoon battles, and Rector eventually was promoted to Vice Squadron Leader of the Second Squadron. Note the typical AVG mix of semi-military clothing and the ever-present cameras and bicycles.

Christman was in the thick of the battles at Rangoon. On 4 January he led one of the Second Squadron flights intercepting a Japanese bombing raid, but was hit by the escorting 77th Sentai 'Nates'. He reported that 'the wings, fuselage, tanks and cockpit of my plane were riddled . . . The engine stopped after five minutes of flying. Smoke came into [the] cockpit and the controls were damaged'. He bailed out. On 20 January he was part of the AVG escort for an attack on forces at Mae Sot, Thailand. They were intercepted and Christman was hit with 27 rounds, including several through the canopy. Three days later he was again hit by the usual swarm of escorting 77th Sentai 'Nates', but this time he did not escape – he was found on the ground shot through the neck with his parachute unopened. Days prior to this, he and Ed Rector had visited a local convent during one of their off-duty sightseeing trips, presumably for a tour, and while there Christman met Dorothea Wilkins. He wrote in her autograph book, under a cartoon of a Tomahawk, 'Dorothea, may the American Sharks of the air keep you safe'. Wilkins attended his funeral, and remembers that it was delayed while the British buried a Japanese airman with full military honours. (*Photo Copyright David Armstrong*)

Christman made pencil sketches for his pilot caricatures, each of course based on a panda bear. The cartoon for 'Scarsdale Jack' Newkirk (above – Tomahawk '34') poked fun at his presumably sophisticated 'Big Apple' lifestyle. Robert 'Moose' Moss (above middle – Tomahawk '39') of Georgia got the predictable hayseed treatment. According to 'Tex' Hill, Pete Wright's 'big butt and pointy nose' were caricatured for Tomahawk '44' (above right). 'Tex' Hill (right – Tomahawk '48') was of course represented by a 'cowboy', while Gil Bright's demonstration of parachuting expertise during training was lampooned for Tomahawk '56' (far right). Several other caricatures were devised, but not all of them had been applied to aircraft by the time of Christman's death (*David Lee Hill via David Armstrong*)

Christman's best known 'nose art' was the 'cycling panda' he painted on Tomahawk '47' to poke fun at the high-speed cycling of Flight Leader John Petach as he raced about to meet his future bride, AVG nurse Emma Jane Foster. Here, Flight Leader Robert Layher gives us not only a good view of Christman's artwork, but of typical AVG warm-weather attire (*Robert Layher*)

first practitioner of individualised 'nose art' in the war. According to 'Tex' Hill and Robert Layher, Christman originally intended to paint these cartoons on all of the Second Squadron's aeroplanes because, as Layher recalls, 'everyone wanted one'. But, given the late start, and the ambitiousness of the plan, only a few were actually completed.

George Bailey recalls seeing Christman painting some of these cartoons 'in two sizes', but he notes that after the squadron was posted to Rangoon on 28 December, there was absolutely no more time for such work. Christman painted John Petach's Tomahawk (number '47') with a small cartoon of a panda bear riding a bicycle to commemorate Petach's speedy bicycling to meet future wife Emma Jane Foster. He also painted a caricature on Frank Swartz's aeroplane (number '49') – 'a cross between a Panda and a mouse orating from a soapbox', according to one wartime account – since Swartz had a reputation for giving speeches on matters of world affairs

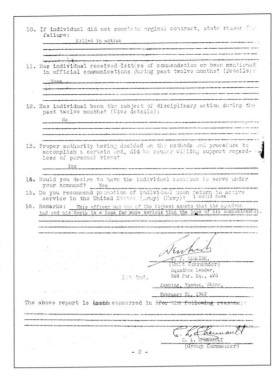

Second Squadron Leader Jack Newkirk's 20 February 1942 report on Christman's death (*Mark Burken*)

to anyone who would listen. Christman also decorated 'Tex' Hill's aeroplane (number '48') with a panda 'cowboy' and steer skull.

In addition to these, Christman created personalised cartoons for the aeroplanes of squadron leader Jack Newkirk (number '34'), Ed Rector (number '36'), Robert Moss (number '39'), Peter Wright (number '44') and Gil Bright (number '56'), but few of these designs were actually placed on the respective aeroplanes by the time the unit was sent to Rangoon. Hill recalls that the design for Rector's machine was definitely not placed on the fighter, and Peter Wright says he didn't even see the sketch of the cartoon for his aeroplane until many years after the war. Christman's favoured location for his cartoons was the starboard fuselage above the trailing edge of the wing. They were small, probably no more than 18 inches in height, and the predominant colours used were black and white.

Only a few AVG aircraft sported other personal insignia. The AVG 'photo-ship' can be seen with a 'swami' head design of unknown authorship on the left front fuselage. Tomahawk '3' had small US (port) and Chinese (starboard) national insignia on either side of the fuselage in front of the cockpit. According to pilot Richard Rossi, these were made with the stencils used to mark AVG ground equipment. Tomahawk '25' had a small cartoon – probably an illustration from a magazine – doped onto the area in front of the cockpit.

When Tomahawk '49' was transferred to Tom Haywood of the Third Squadron in April or May 1942 it still featured Christman's 'orating panda' cartoon, and Haywood added a bulldog head insignia on both sides of the fuselage. Several aircraft in the Third Squadron had 'meatball' kill markings added beginning in January 1942. These were always on the port side near the cockpit in a simple red disc/white rectangle style. These were not added until mid-January 1942.

INTO ACTION

E vents elsewhere in Asia put a sudden halt to concerns about fancy paint work. As AVG Commander Claire Chennault climbed down from the crude control tower at Kyedaw airfield on the morning of Monday, 8 December 1941, an excited radioman ran up waving the news of the attack on Pearl Harbor. The field was immediately put on alert and the squadrons ordered to stand by.

First Squadron Flight Leader Charles Bond points to the hole from a 7.7 mm round following the AVG's combat baptism at Kunming on 20 December 1941. Bond got into action by borrowing this aeroplane when his own was unserviceable, and he was credited with assisting in the destruction of one of the ten bombers credited to the AVG. He was appointed Vice Squadron Leader on 21 April, and was credited with 8.77 victories in an eventful AVG tour. Bond volunteered to serve two extra weeks in China after the AVG disbanded, and then rejoined the USAAF, scoring three additional victories. He remained in the service as a career officer postwar, retiring with the rank of major general (*Charles R Bond, Jr*)

ROBERT NEALE

Robert Neale was Vice Leader of the First Squadron at the time this photo (right) was taken of him on the wing of his assigned aircraft, Tomahawk number '7', at Kunming in January 1942. Neale was a dive-bomber pilot aboard the *Saratoga* when he was recruited for the AVG. He was involved in the group's first combat on 20 December at Kunming, although he admitted that he had no idea if he had shot down, or even hit, any of the enemy bombers. Neale got his first official victory on 23 January. On 7 February First Squadron Leader Sandy Sandell was killed when testing a rebuilt aeroplane and Neale was appointed Squadron Leader – a job he did not relish. Despite this, he ably led the squadron during the exhausting battles in the weeks that followed, and

was in action continuously from 12 January to 13 March, logging 64 combat flying hours in February alone. By the time the AVG was disbanded, he was America's highest-scoring ace, credited with 15.55 kills. Neale volunteered to remain in China for two extra weeks as temporary Commander of the 23rd FG. He had lost 40 lbs, and was 'gaunt, bony and hollow-eyed' from illness and the continuous pressure. He was offered the rank of major in the USAAF, but declined it, and returned to the US, where he flew with American Overseas Airlines until he retired in 1950. Regarding his AVG experience, Neale once said, 'I've never been a hero type, and I wasn't figuring on starting then, if ever'.
(*Photo Copyright Jack Cook via Carl Molesworth*)

At least two different airframes wore number '7' as Robert Neale's assigned aircraft. This photograph, almost certainly taken at Kunming in January 1942, shows the first. The serial number of this fighter was believed to be P-8146 (*Jack Cook via Carl Molesworth*)

First Squadron Tomahawk '18' has its guns bore-sighted probably at Kunming in January 1942. AVG armourers actually fired-in the guns. Wing guns were usually charged and locked before flight, while the fuselage guns were charged in the air before combat (*Don Rodewald via Frank Losonsky*)

Chennault designated the 'Hell's Angels' as the 'assault echelon', while the Second and First Pursuit Squadrons were respectively designated the 'support' and 'reserve' echelons. Chennault also appointed Third Squadron Leader Arvid Olson as 'Group Commander in the Air'. On 10 December Thailand effectively became an ally of the Japanese. With the AVG base at Toungoo only a short flight from Thai airfields, and not covered by the Chinese warning net he had so carefully cultivated, Chennault's immediate concern was to avoid being caught on the ground in a surprise attack.

A photo-reconnaissance mission was mounted by Erik Shilling, escorted by Bert Christman and Ed Rector. The pictures revealed a massive build-up of Japanese air strength in Thailand. Chennault had no bombers for a pre-emptive strike, however. After much wrangling between Chennault, Commonwealth commanders, and Chiang, it was decided

Although of poor quality, this is the only known photograph of Tomahawk '23' (probably P-8188), which was assigned to William 'Black Mac' McGarry. Note the 'dimples' and the toned-down side number. McGarry, a former Army P-40 pilot at Selfridge Field, was one of the AVG's most successful pilots during the Rangoon battles. However, while participating in the attack on the Japanese air base at Chiang Mai, in Thailand, on 24 March 1942 he was hit by anti-aircraft fire and forced to bail out. He was captured by Thai forces and turned over to the Japanese. He was interrogated by none other than Maj Tateo Kato, Commander of the 64th Sentai. The Japanese gave him back to the Thais, who held him in a Bangkok jail until his escape in May 1944. McGarry was credited with 10.29 victories in the AVG (*Ben Levario*)

According to the photographer, Third Squadron Armorer Chuck Baisden, this shot of Flight Leader Robert 'Duke' Hedman – apparently in Tomahawk '68' – was taken on 25 December 1941. Hedman, a former P-40 pilot in the Army Air Corps, was credited with destroying four Ki-21 'Sallys' and one Ki-43 'Oscar' on this date, thus becoming America's first 'ace in a day'. Following this mission, Hedman suggested that it would be fairer if CAMCO divided all credited kills on the mission among the participating pilots, since each shared some credit for the final result. With a bookkeeping error added for good measure, he ended up with 3.83 official kills rather than 5. He later added one more victory for an official total of 4.83. He is reported to have said after the Rangoon battles that he would make no further claims because it was 'bad luck to count them'. Hedman was one of the few AVG pilots at Loiwing in April 1942 who declined to threaten resignation during the 'job action' Chennault called the 'pilots' revolt'. After the AVG disbanded, he flew transports with the China National Airways Corporation (*Chuck Baisden*)

that one AVG squadron would assist the RAF's No 67 Sqn in the defence at Rangoon, while the other two would be deployed to Kunming. On 12 December the Third Squadron was despatched to Mingaladon. It had been allocated a total of 31 aircraft since training began, but by 1 December it had 23 aircraft on charge. At the time of its first combat on 23 December, only 18 Tomahawks were in service, and 14 were put in the air for its baptism of fire.

The First and Second Squadrons moved to Kunming on 18 December, and most of their support personnel were flown up the next day. This movement went surprisingly well, considering that the AVG had neither accurate maps nor direction-finding equipment at its disposal. Simple cross-country flights were hazardous in this part of the world, and other such flights were not so lucky. The First and Second Squadrons had 34 aircraft between them. Twelve unserviceable machines were left at Kyedaw, which was used as an auxiliary field and Group Engineering station throughout the Rangoon campaign. Meanwhile, as much war material as possible was being despatched up the Burma Road from Rangoon.

The Japanese had just resumed attacks on Kunming a few days before the 'Adam and Eves' and 'Panda Bears' arrived. On 20 December they sent ten unescorted bombers as a sacrificial 'discarding stones squadron' to test the defences and entice re-deployment of Allied air strength northward. The mission had no effect on Allied deployments, but its sacrificial nature

Chinese-American Engineering helpers stand next to newly-repainted Tomahawk '75' at Wu Chia Ba airfield, Kunming, in mid-January 1942. Frank Losonsky recalls that they were likely Chun Yuen Gee, Pak On Lee, George Lum, Kee Jeung Pan, George Wing Shee, Lem Fong Wu and Francis Yee, all from Group Engineering. Compare these markings with those on Tomahawk '75' in the photographs (on pages 33 and 34) shot at Toungoo in December 1941 (*Frank Losonsky*)

Third Squadron pilot Paul J Greene in front of his assigned Tomahawk number '84' at Kunming in early 1942. Green was serving as an Army Air Corps flight instructor with R T Smith at Randolph Field when he joined the AVG. In the 'Hell's Angels'' first action, he was credited with shooting down a 77th Sentai 'Nate', but was himself shot down. He was strafed in his parachute, but survived by dumping air to hasten his descent. While at Loiwing in April 1942, Greene was credited with shooting down a Ki-43. After the AVG disbanded he returned to the US and rejoined the Army Air Forces. After a tour as Director of Gunnery Training at Madigan Air Base, he was appointed CO of the 97th FS at Foggia, in Italy, and flew 50 missions in P-38s. Greene was credited with two victories by CAMCO (*R T Smith via Brad Smith*)

Greene's handiwork on Tomahawk '84', again seen in early 1942. Note the characteristic Third Squadron striping details (*R T Smith via Brad Smith*)

Flight Leader Bill Reed pops his ears before taking off in Tomahawk '74' from Kunming in early 1942. Note the faint remains of the number under the cockpit (*Frank Losonsky*)

was better realised when the raid was intercepted by Chennault's shark-faced Tomahawks.

One of the Japanese pilots, Gouichi Suzuki, recalled for TV cameras years later that his unit did not have much experience in air combat, but he felt this was 'a very harsh' mission. He remembered that the enemy interceptors 'came right at us. They flew so close to us that we could see their faces'. Although he recognised the insignia as Chinese, 'it was clear that the pilots were American because they were brave enough to come in such close quarters'. He recalls that three of his comrades went down over China. Suzuki limped back to his base near Hanoi with about 30 holes in his own aeroplane and two dead crewmen, noting that 'lots' of the returning aeroplanes had to belly-in or land on one wheel.

Most importantly for the fledgling AVG, the raiders never reached Kunming, and the Japanese would make no further attacks on the city while the AVG was there.

43

Flight Leader Tom Haywood is seen on the wing in Tomahawk '94' over Kunming in early 1942 (*R T Smith via Brad Smith*)

Haywood contemplates the squadron's aeroplane and engine status board at Kunming in early 1942 (*R T Smith via Brad Smith*)

This January 1942 photo of R T Smith and his assigned aircraft clearly shows the freshly-repainted markings and repairs on the wing. One of Smith's most memorable air combats occurred on 10 April 1942 near Loiwing, when his flight tangled with 64th Sentai 'Oscars' led by two of the Imperial Army's top pilots, Tateo Kato and Yohei Hinoki. Smith shot down one Ki-43 and damaged another. In 1992 he learned that the enemy fighter he had damaged had been flown by Hinoki, whom he had seriously wounded with two rounds. Hinoki barely made it back to perform a dead-stick landing at his base at Chiang Mai, Thailand. He was hospitalised for a month, and out of action for many more. Smith was officially credited with 8.73 victories in the AVG, all achieved in aerial combat (*R T Smith via Brad Smith*)

R T Smith hams it up at Kunming in January 1942. After the AVG disbanded, Smith returned to the US for another stint as a flight instructor, before returning to the CBI to serve in Phil Cochran's 1st Air Commando Group, ultimately as CO of the group's B-25H unit. One of his most important missions was the famous March 1944 photo-reconnaissance flight that discovered the obstructed glider landing ground at the 'Piccadilly' field during Operation *Thursday*. He may have gained more notoriety though for buzzing Theatre Commander Lord Louis Mountbatten as he gave a pep talk to the group! After the war, he worked as a pilot for TWA before becoming a writer for television and radio shows like 'Hopalong Cassidy' and 'Lum 'n' Abner'. After that he worked for Lockheed, and finally became Vice President Far East for the Flying Tiger Line, before retiring. He was once asked if he ever regretted joining the AVG, and he replied 'Only on those occasions when I was being shot at' (*R T Smith via Brad Smith*)

A Second Squadron Tomahawk takes off in a cloud of dust at Mingaladon in late January 1942 to intercept bombers. This shot was taken by Pulitzer Prize-winning photographer George Rodger. Close examination of the original print indicates that this is probably Squadron Leader John Newkirk's Tomahawk '34'. Newkirk, a Navy fighter pilot, led his squadron during the AVG's first combat at Kunming on 20 December although, as AVG Commander Claire Chennault put it, he experienced 'buck fever' and ordered his flight to break off before contact, leaving the job to the First Squadron. He led the 'Panda Bears' to Rangoon on 28 December 1941, where he had more success, including the destruction of Ki-27 'Nates' on 8 and 20 January. During the 23 January interception at Rangoon, he was credited with another victory, but was badly shot up and had to crash-land himself. With an eerie foreboding, Newkirk led part of the Chiang Mai strafing attack on 24 March and was shot down and killed by ground fire. He was credited with 10.5 kills by CAMCO (*Copyright George Rodger*)

Understandably, after years of indiscriminate bombing the Chinese were overjoyed at this turn of events.

But the main theatre of action was to be Burma, and the battle for Rangoon began on 23 December. There, the Third Squadron and Commonwealth air forces – and later the rest of the AVG as well – would battle the biggest air armadas yet seen in Asia. The odds were so long that while the 'Hell's Angels' had substantial success in what R T Smith called 'on-the-job training to the utmost', this came with a steady toll in lives and equipment. The Japanese attacked with 100+ bombers and fighters on the 23rd, and 14 Tomahawks and 16 Buffaloes rose to intercept. Two AVG pilots were shot down and killed, two more went missing and three more aeroplanes were damaged. Six Japanese aircraft were claimed in exchange.

Ken Jernstedt recalled that 'what enthusiasm we had for the victories was dimmed considerably by the fact that we'd lost two good men'. No 67 Sqn, although faring much better than other Allied fighter squadrons in the first months of the Pacific War, was less successful than the AVG.

Japanese bombing also did considerable damage to Rangoon and Mingaladon aerodrome. Armorer Chuck Baisden dove for the slit trenches as the bombs fell – 'that's when I got personally acquainted with the war', he said. 'I was scared, my God, I was scared'.

JAMES HOWARD

Second Squadron pilots are seen at Mingaladon in this photo (right), taken in late January 1942. They are, front from left to right, Squadron Leader John Newkirk, Henry Geselbracht and Flight Leader James Howard. Behind them are pilots William Bartling and Robert Layher. Howard was born in Canton, China, of missionary parents, and was a fighter pilot on the *Saratoga* when he signed up as a Flight Leader with the AVG. His first big mission was the 3 January 1942 dawn strafing attack on the fighter base at Tak, in Thailand. He was credited with the destruction of four aircraft on the ground, but almost bailed out when his engine momentarily quit. After serving at Rangoon, Howard was appointed Group Operations Officer and ordered to assist in preparing new bases in China. By early May he was promoted to squadron leader status and back in the air. The promotion meant only a pay raise, however, since there were no vacant squadron leader positions at the time. On the AVG's last day of operations he claimed a 'Nate' for a total score of 6.33. Howard volunteered for two extra weeks in China with the 23rd FG, then joined the Army Air Forces and was posted to Europe. There, he commanded the 354th FG and scored seven more victories to become one of a handful of aces in both

theatres. Howard received the Medal of Honor for 'conspicuous gallantry and intrepidity above and beyond the call of duty' for his actions near Oschersleben, Germany on 11 January 1944 when, in order to protect a hard-pressed bomber formation, he 'chose to attack single-handed a formation of more than 30 German aeroplanes. With utter disregard for his own safety he immediately pressed home determined attacks for some 30 minutes, during which time he destroyed 3 enemy aeroplanes and probably destroyed and damaged others'. When later asked by the press about this incident, he simply said, 'I seen my duty and I done it'.
(*Photo Copyright George Rodger*)

Armorer Joe Poshefko remembers driving to the airfield after the bombing attack had ended and finding that 'there were bombs all over the place'. The enemy had just 'bombed at will'. On Christmas Day the Imperial Army Air Force returned with over 150 aircraft. Third Squadron Leader Arvid Olson put 13 Tomahawks in the air to oppose them, and No 67 Sqn intercepted with 14 Buffaloes. Results were considerably better this time, with combined AVG and RAF claims for the destruction of 25 Japanese aircraft.

Third Squadron pilot Charles Older recalled that enemy aeroplanes 'were dropping like flies. They were rolling out of the formation, wings coming off, blowing up. It was a scene like something out of hell'. No 'Hell's Angels' pilots were lost, but two aircraft were wrecked and, worse, four RAF pilots were killed. By that time the Third Squadron had

ED RECTOR

Second Squadron Flight Leader Ed Rector prepares to scramble from Mingaladon to intercept a Japanese bombing raid (right) in late January 1942. Number '52' is just visible above the eye of the shark head. Rector was a dive-bomber pilot on the *Ranger* when he volunteered for the AVG. On 20 December he decided on his own initiative to join the First Squadron interception of the Japanese bombing raid on Kunming. Although he shared in the credited victories, he had to belly-in his aircraft when he ran out of fuel. On 24 January he was credited with the destruction of a Ki-27 'Nate' and a Ki-21 'Sally'. On 19 April he shot down a Japanese reconnaissance aircraft, and five days later he helped shoot down another. By May Rector had been promoted to vice squadron leader and, flying a Kittyhawk, led many of the missions in support of Chinese forces near the Salween River gorge. He led a number of other important escort and strike missions in May and June, and on 4 July scored his last victory as a member of the AVG, bringing his official total to 6.52. After the AVG disbanded Rector joined the Army Air Forces and was appointed CO of the 76th FS/23rd FG. He rose to the rank of colonel, and CO of the 23rd FG, and on 2 April 1945 he scored the last aerial victory with the 23rd FG for a career total of 10.75.
(*Photo Copyright George Rodger*)

First Squadron Flight Leader Bill Bartling at Mingaladon on 29 January 1942. Bartling often flew as Squadron Leader Bob Neale's wingman, beginning with the AVG's first combat on 20 December. On 24 January he was credited with the destruction of one Ki-27 'Nate', but had to crash-land after having his control cables shot out. He was credited with the destruction of another 'Nate' near Rangoon on 28 January, and participated in the Moulmein strafing attack on 24 February. Bartling also participated in the Chiang Mai strafing attack on 24 March. On 9 May he shot down a Ki-46 'Dinah' recce aeroplane flying some 27,000 ft over Kunming – probably the AVG's highest altitude combat. Bartling volunteered to extend his CAMCO contract for two extra weeks in order to help the 23rd FG get started, then became a transport pilot for CNAC. He was officially credited with 7.27 kills in the AVG (*Copyright George Rodger*)

11 aeroplanes left, only six of which were immediately serviceable. Meanwhile, news correspondents and photographers began to arrive and produce the only positive news copy coming out of the Allied war effort in the Pacific. And these vivid accounts would, for the first time, refer to this rough and ready group of 'civilian' volunteers as the 'Flying Tigers'.

After receiving reports of the Rangoon fights, Chennault decided to withdraw the Third Squadron to Kunming, and despatch the Second in its place. The 'Panda Bears' arrived in Rangoon with 18 fresh aircraft on 30 December. The 'Hell's Angels' flew away ten aircraft and left behind several that could not be made airworthy. The Second Squadron got right to work with pre-emptive strafing attacks on Japanese airfields.

But the Japanese were able to maintain their overwhelming superiority in numbers despite alarmingly heavy losses. They increased the number of fighters escorting their bomber formations, started to send fighter sweeps, and finally switched the emphasis of bombing operations to night raids. On 12 January the invasion of Burma

began and by 31 January, Commonwealth forces had withdrawn from Moulmein and the rest of the southern Burmese province of Tenasserim.

The Imperial Army Air Force's vastly superior numbers were slowly grinding up meagre Allied air assets, and while AVG morale remained high, by the end of January only some ten Tomahawks remained serviceable at Mingaladon. Second Squadron Leader Jack Newkirk reported to Chennault on 28 January that the 'aeroplanes that we have here now are beginning to look like patchwork quilts for the holes in them. The engines are also getting tired . . . There are not sufficient groundcrews for the job, and there is not enough time for them to teach the Chinese or other helpers which they steal from our neighbours . . .'

No 67 Sqn had lost eight pilots and eight aeroplanes since combat began, although a few No 17 Sqn Hurricanes (*text continues on page 65*)

A Second Squadron Tomahawk is seen after returning to Mingaladon following an interception mission in late January 1942. Most First and Second Squadron shark heads were stylistically similar – at first glance the shark head appears identical to that seen previously on Tomahawk '52', but closer inspection reveals subtle differences in placement and details (*Copyright George Rodger*)

Communications man Alex 'Mickey' Mihalko and pilots John Petach and Gil Bright are seen in the chow line at Mingaladon. Note their distinctly non-military floral pattern plates. Mihalko was in charge of AVG communications at Rangoon despite bouts of illness and a lack of essential equipment. The RAF command had the only radar set in Burma, and its operators did not communicate directly with the AVG. So Mihalko's communications work consisted primarily of lurking about the RAF command centre and 'intercepting' the radar signals and telephoning the AVG alert tent with the news! As a result, the AVG often got off faster than their allies did, although adequate warning and ground control were a constant problem. Mihalko was one of only three AVG ground personnel to be decorated with the Chinese Cloud Banner, and after the AVG disbanded, he re-enlisted in the Navy in China (*Copyright George Rodger*)

COLOUR PLATES

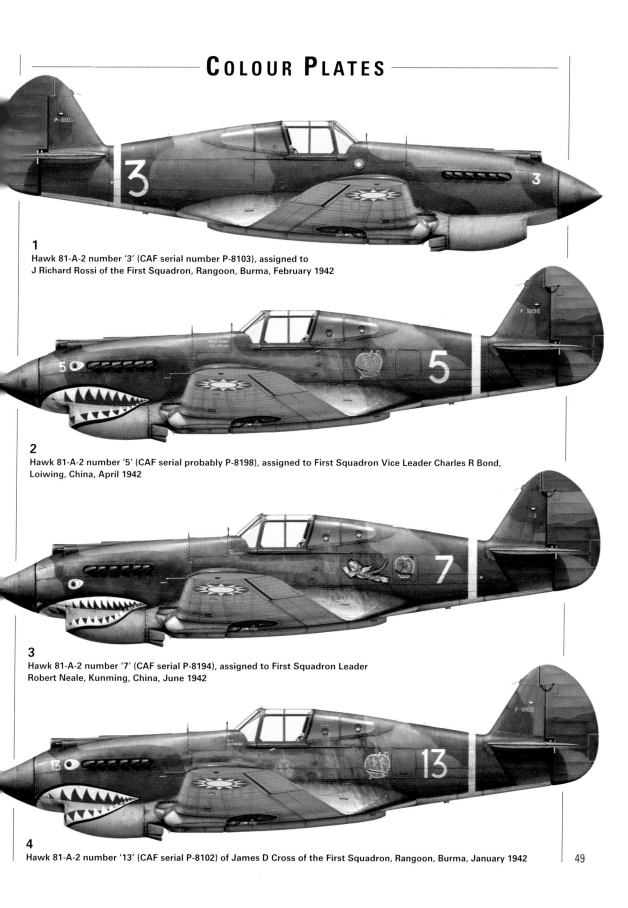

1
Hawk 81-A-2 number '3' (CAF serial number P-8103), assigned to
J Richard Rossi of the First Squadron, Rangoon, Burma, February 1942

2
Hawk 81-A-2 number '5' (CAF serial probably P-8198), assigned to First Squadron Vice Leader Charles R Bond,
Loiwing, China, April 1942

3
Hawk 81-A-2 number '7' (CAF serial P-8194), assigned to First Squadron Leader
Robert Neale, Kunming, China, June 1942

4
Hawk 81-A-2 number '13' (CAF serial P-8102) of James D Cross of the First Squadron, Rangoon, Burma, January 1942

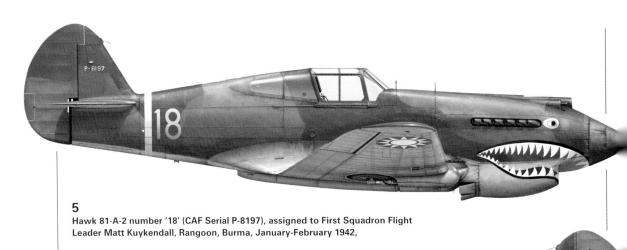

5
Hawk 81-A-2 number '18' (CAF Serial P-8197), assigned to First Squadron Flight
Leader Matt Kuykendall, Rangoon, Burma, January-February 1942,

6
Hawk 81-A-2 number '21' (CAF serial P-8182), assigned to First Squadron Vice Squadron Leaders Frank Schiel and
Greg 'Pappy' Boyington, Rangoon, Burma, January-February 1942

7
Hawk 81-A-2 number '25' (CAF serial P-8144), assigned to Einar 'Mickey' Mickelson of the First Squadron,
Rangoon, Burma, January 1942

8
Hawk 81-A-2 number '33' (CAF serial P-8151) of First Squadron Flight Leader Robert Little, Kunming, China, April 1942

9
Hawk 81-A-2 number '34' (CAF Serial P-8196), assigned to Second Squadron Leader John Newkirk, Toungoo, Burma, December 1941

10
Hawk 81-A-2 number '36' (CAF serial P-8123), assigned to Second Squadron Vice Leader Edward Rector, Rangoon, Burma, January-February 1942

11
Hawk 81-A-2 number '44' (CAF Serial P-8184), assigned to Second Squadron Flight Leader Peter Wright, Rangoon, Burma, January 1942

12
Hawk 81-A-2 number '45' (CAF Serial P-8165) of Percy Bartelt of the Second Squadron, Kunming, China, March 1942

13
Hawk 81-A-2 number '47' (CAF serial P-8127), assigned to Second Squadron Flight Leader John Petach, Rangoon, Burma, January-February 1942

14
Hawk 81-A-2 number '47' (CAF serial P-8127), assigned to Robert T Smith of the Third Squadron, Kunming, China, June 1942

15
Hawk 81-A-2 number '48' (CAF serial P-8134), assigned to David Lee 'Tex' Hill of the Second Squadron, Toungoo, Burma, December 1941

16
Hawk 81-A-2 number '49' (CAF serial P-8133) of Tom Haywood of the Third Squadron, Kunming, China, May-June 1942

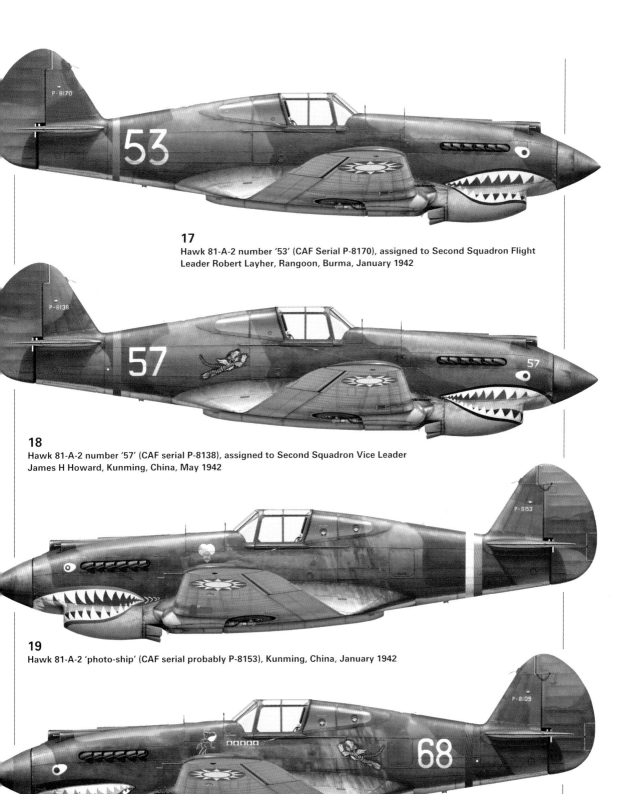

17
Hawk 81-A-2 number '53' (CAF Serial P-8170), assigned to Second Squadron Flight Leader Robert Layher, Rangoon, Burma, January 1942

18
Hawk 81-A-2 number '57' (CAF serial P-8138), assigned to Second Squadron Vice Leader James H Howard, Kunming, China, May 1942

19
Hawk 81-A-2 'photo-ship' (CAF serial probably P-8153), Kunming, China, January 1942

20
Hawk 81-A-2 number '68' (CAF serial P-8109), assigned to Third Squadron Flight Leader Charles Older, Kunming, China, early May 1942

21
Hawk 81-A-2 number '69' (CAF serial P-8115), assigned to Neil Martin and then Lewis Bishop, both from the Third Squadron, Kunming, China, March 1942

22
Hawk 81-A-2 Number '71' (CAF Serial P-8119), assigned to Ed Overend of the Third Squadron, Kunming, China, March 1942

23
Hawk 81-A-2 number '75' (CAF serial P-8186), assigned to Third Squadron Flight Leader William Reed, Kunming, China, January 1942

24
Hawk 81-A-2 number '77' (CAF serial P-8173) of Third Squadron Flight Leader R T Smith, Kunming, China, January 1942

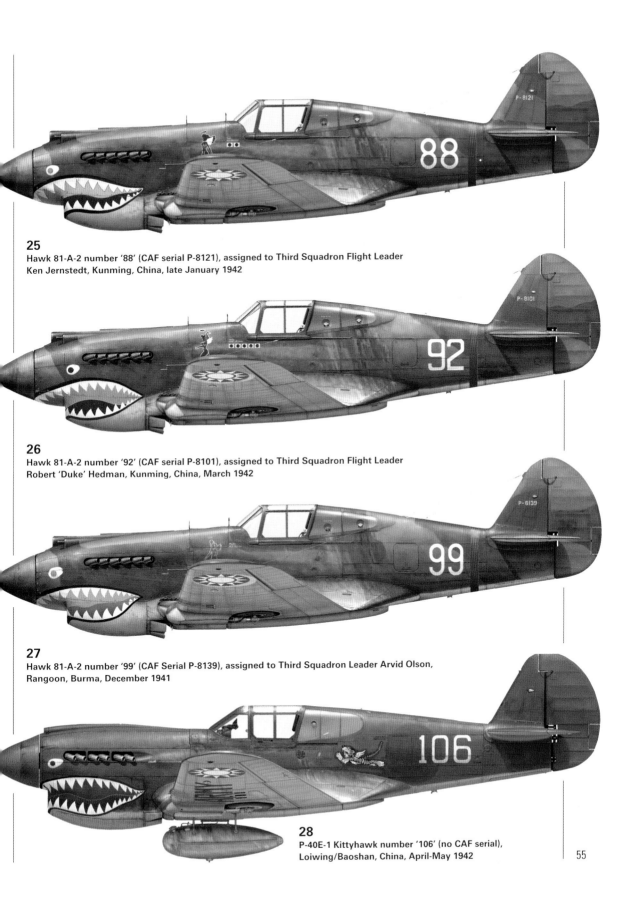

25
Hawk 81-A-2 number '88' (CAF serial P-8121), assigned to Third Squadron Flight Leader
Ken Jernstedt, Kunming, China, late January 1942

26
Hawk 81-A-2 number '92' (CAF serial P-8101), assigned to Third Squadron Flight Leader
Robert 'Duke' Hedman, Kunming, China, March 1942

27
Hawk 81-A-2 number '99' (CAF Serial P-8139), assigned to Third Squadron Leader Arvid Olson,
Rangoon, Burma, December 1941

28
P-40E-1 Kittyhawk number '106' (no CAF serial),
Loiwing/Baoshan, China, April-May 1942

Upper plan view of Tomahawk '77', showing the camouflage pattern used on nearly all AVG Tomahawks. These shades were applied with the aid of rubber mats, insuring sharp demarcations and uniformity

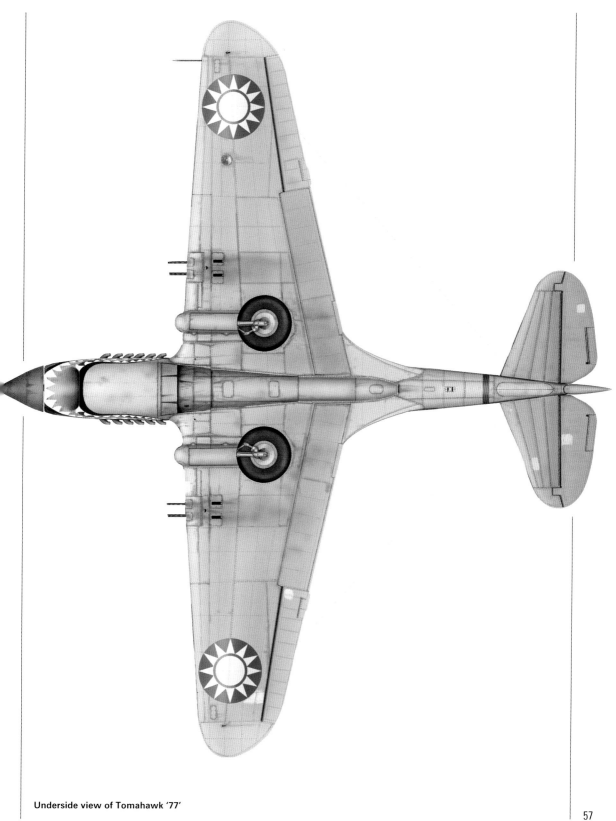

Underside view of Tomahawk '77'

Scrap view 1
Cartoon version of the 'First Pursuit' insignia and tiger decal applied to the starboard side on Tomahawk '7'

Scrap view 2
First Pursuit 'Adam and Eve' insignia on Tomahawk '13'

Scrap view 3
Bert Christman's cartoon of 'Scarsdale Jack', which may have decorated Tomahawk '34'

Scrap view 4
Bert Christman's 'cycling panda' that adorned Tomahawk '47'

Scrap view 5
The 'horned bulldog' added by Third Squadron personnel to Tomahawk '49'

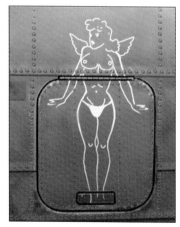

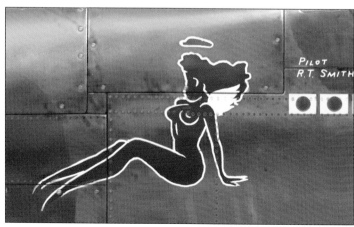

Scrap view 6
The port detail view of the chalk or water-paint 'Hell's Angel' insignia hastily applied to Tomahawk P-8115 in September 1941

Scrap view 7
'Hell's Angel' insignia on Tomahawk '77'

Scrap view 8
'Flying Tiger' decal received by the AVG in March 1942. The blue 'V-for-Victory' element of the decal was not always used

Scrap view 9
The blue-lipped shark head on Tomahawk '36'

Scrap view 10
The shark head on Tomahawk '77', as revised in January 1942

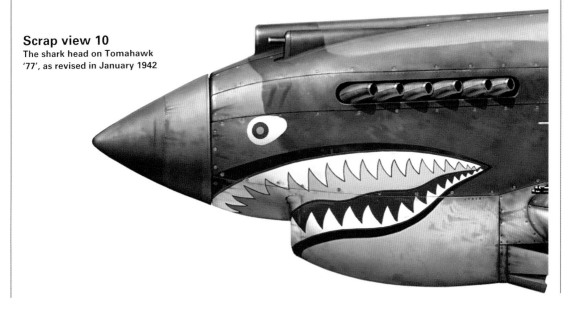

Scrap View 11

Examples of Third Squadron 'Hell's Angels'. These adorned the Tomahawks assigned to Ken Jernstedt (top left – aircraft '88'), Charles Older (centre – aircraft '68'), Bill Reed (top right – aircraft '75') and Arvid Olson (bottom left – aircraft '99'). The figure at bottom right is an often-seen pose probably not painted by Stanley Regis

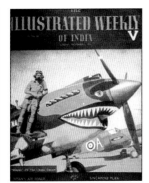

1

2

3

4

5

6

7

8

9

10

11

12

13

14

15

16

17   **18**

This George Rodger photo of the commercial table radio and telephone that comprised the AVG communications 'system' during the Rangoon campaign provides a telling example of the Allies' early improvised war in Asia. Here, Flight Leader John Petach is seen tuning the radio for useful news. A former Navy pilot, Petach scored a fraction over two victories during the Rangoon battles, and was credited with a total of 3.98 kills before the AVG disbanded on 4 July. He then volunteered to stay in China two extra weeks and served as a flight leader in the 75th FS, scoring one additional victory on 6 July. However, while on a bombing mission to Linchuan on 10 July he was hit by ground fire and died instantly when his aeroplane blew up. He was belatedly awarded the US Distinguished Flying Cross in 1984 for his conduct during his six days of service with the 75th FS (*Copyright George Rodger*)

had recently arrived. Chennault started sending reinforcements from the 'Adam and Eves'. Eight pilots and their aeroplanes were sent first, and the 'Panda Bears' were then progressively withdrawn to Kunming.

Damaged aircraft, meanwhile, were being shuttled to Toungoo and Kunming for major repairs. But no one could have expected such small forces to carry the fight at Rangoon for long without substantial reinforcements, and there were none available. Second Squadron pilot 'Tex' Hill commented years later for a TV documentary that the AVG simply did not have the assets to sustain operations long enough to really 'attrition' enemy forces – 'we'd fight until we'd lose our combat effectiveness and then we'd have to move back to a rear area and regroup and put the aeroplanes back together and go again'. Chennault was clearly stretching his limited resources as far as he dared.

Despite the trickle of reinforcements, and a surprising break in Japanese activity, in mid February Newkirk reported that he possessed just ten airworthy Tomahawks at Mingaladon, with ten others unserviceable. A few weeks later he was reporting (probably about combined Second and First Squadron equipment rotated to his command) that 25 Tomahawks could be put into commission, and of these, 17 were 'now ready and in use', while five more were being repaired at Toungoo. Six others needed major repairs, two would be flown to Kunming for overhaul and the others were 'write-offs'.

First Squadron Flight Leader Charles Bond noted in his diary on 25 February that 'we are flying aircraft that would be condemned back in the States'. Commonwealth forces, meanwhile, could muster about a dozen Hurricanes and Buffaloes, a handful of Blenheims and other even less combat-capable types. This motley Allied force confronted an enemy that was in fact growing in strength as new units and replacements were rotated into the area.

By the end of February the 'Panda Bears' were nearly exhausted, a fact reflected not only in depleted equipment but also in discipline and conduct problems. Bond noted in his diary that 'We do things over here that would surely draw court-martials at home'. But more significantly, Allied ground forces were in retreat and Rangoon was in danger of encirclement.

Communications with RAF forces had never been good, with AVG pilots seldom getting more than a ten-minute warning of an incoming raid. Then, on 27 February, the AVG discovered that the RAF had pulled out its radar equipment and was retreating north to Magwe. Remaining First and Second Squadron personnel and aeroplanes were withdrawn to Kunming. While the aeroplanes and most of the pilots were flown away, most AVG groundcrewmen had to make the trip on the Burma Road, now packed with frightened refugees.

Despite the situation rapidly deteriorating, George Tyrell had married the daughter of the Rangoon dock manager! He spent his honeymoon driving up the Burma Road with his bride in the car they had received

Ex-Navy pilot Frank 'Whitey' Lawlor returns from an interception at Mingaladon in late January 1942. Note his oil-stained pant legs, a characteristic of AVG pilots. Lawlor claimed four Ki-27s on 23 January, and became an ace six days later following the destruction of another 'Nate'. He also participated in the Chiang Mai attack, and on 5 May downed two 11th Sentai 'Nates' near Baoshan. He also participated in the attacks at the Salween River Gorge, and finished his AVG service with 8.5 kills. He then rejoined the Navy (*Copyright George Rodger*)

from her father as a wedding gift. They refuelled at Chinese gasoline dumps and used canned peaches to barter accommodations along the way. George Bailey was part of the last large AVG convoy to leave Rangoon. He drove a newly-liberated Buick while others drove commandeered Plymouths and International trucks. The drive took 19 days, but they lost only one truck.

Frank Andersen found an abandoned truck loaded with ammunition on the Rangoon docks. Using the improvisational ability that characterised AVG groundcrewmen, he ejected the ammunition into the harbour and turned the vehicle over to the man who, with his three daughters, had managed one of the AVG's favourite night-spots. They made their escape to India with it.

Crew Chief Irving Stolet had been working at the Group Engineering unit at Toungoo, itself increasingly untenable as the Rangoon campaign reached its climax. During those last days he found himself driving a truck to pick up a wrecked aeroplane for repair. After learning of Rangoon's imminent fall he returned to Kyedaw field, which was being bombed 'night and day'. He volunteered to drive the next truck north. Another vehicle accompanied him, but it soon disappeared and

RAF and AVG personnel examine the wreckage of a 77th Sentai Nakajima Ki-27 'Nate' at Mingaladon probably on 29 January 1942. The pilot had tried to crash his damaged fighter into a parked Blenheim bomber (*Copyright George Rodger*)

Second Squadron pilot Tom Cole was photographed at Mingaladon on 29 January 1942. Cole was a Navy PBY pilot when he joined the AVG. He shot down a 'Nate' on 24 January but was killed the day after this shot was taken while on a strafing mission near Moulmein. He was either hit by flak or crashed due to 'target fixation' (*Copyright George Rodger*)

Then-Flight Leader 'Tex' Hill confers with AVG ground staff outside the alert tent in late January 1942 (*Copyright George Rodger*)

Hill and Armorer Jim Musick have a smoke in the alert tent between missions. Note the phone close at hand (*Copyright George Rodger*)

Left
Second Squadron pilots examine the now-removed rudder from the crashed 'Nate' for the benefit of George Rodger's camera. They are, from left to right David Lee 'Tex' Hill, Noel Bacon, Tom Cole, Ed Rector, Frank Lawlor and, just visible, Frank Schiel (*Copyright George Rodger*)

Stolet drove on alone, encountering only crowds of refugees impeding his progress. He stopped at Chinese fuel dumps every hundred miles or so, and crossed the Salween River just before they blew the bridge. Not having seen another American since leaving Toungoo, he rolled into Kunming 21 days later.

Everyone else at Toungoo had been flown out and arrived much earlier, wondering what happened to him. He says that after this trip, life in China seemed 'very pleasant.' Others had similar adventures. Peter Wright's most vivid recollections are not of aerial combat, but his drive up the Burma Road in the closing days of the Burma fighting. Third Squadron Crew Chief Gail McCallister would have one of the most exciting trips of all when he narrowly escaped the advancing Japanese on foot.

MINOR MIRACLES OF REPAIR

Aware of the severe problems confronting the AVG, US Army observers thought the group would last only a few weeks in combat. Had it not been for the efforts of the groundcrews, this prediction might have proved correct. Second squadron ace Ed Rector remarked that the pilots got all the glory, but they were 'nothing compared to the groundcrew personnel,

67

GEORGE BURGARD

This photo (right), probably taken at Mingaladon in February 1942, is one of a very few shots that show a group of First Squadron pilots. They are, from left to right, Squadron Leader Robert Neale, George T Burgard, Flight Leader Robert L Little, Flight Leader Charles Bond, John E Blackburn III and William D McGarry. Note the hastily painted upper lip on the aeroplane's shark head, likely due to replacement of the side cowl

panel. George Burgard was a Ferry Command pilot when he joined the AVG. He was in the thick of the First Squadron's actions at Rangoon, then later assisted in ferrying aircraft from India before being posted with the squadron to Guilin in late May. On his first day there he shot down a 'Nate', then attacked one of the Ki-45 'Nicks' that were making their combat debut. Surprised by its speed and manoeuvrability, he finally shot it down after a long low-level chase. Burgard was credited by CAMCO with 10.79 kills. After the AVG disbanded he became a pilot for American Export Airlines, then transporting war materiel for the Navy. Bob Little was a veteran of the Army Air Corps 8th Pursuit Group, and one of only a few 'Flying Tigers' who had actually flown

P-40s prior to joining the AVG, having 375 hours in the type. He was credited with aerial victories over Ki-27s on 29 January and 6, 25 and 26 February, and with the destruction of a Ki-43 on 8 April. He was killed on 22 May 1942 (by flak or a premature bomb detonation) while flying a Kittyhawk on a ground attack mission against Japanese troops near the Salween River Gorge. Little's final score was 10.55. His loss was a heavy blow to the AVG, and Squadron Leader Robert Neale later told author Robert Hotz that 'Bob flew more missions over enemy territory than anybody else in the outfit. He never turned down a chance to fight. Bob was one of the most aggressive pilots in the AVG and a helluva good guy'. (*Photo Copyright Charles R Bond, Jr*)

because without those people we would never have shot down an aeroplane. It is beyond belief what they accomplished'.

Second Squadron pilot James Howard told an interviewer that it was the groundcrews who 'really kept us alive', and others have remarked on what First Squadron

pilot George Burgard called the 'minor miracles of repair' performed by these men.

Group Engineering was responsible for major overhauls and rebuilding work, but it was the heavy repair work done by AVG crew chiefs in the open on the flightlines that kept the group in business from day to day. Frank Losonsky recalls changing landing gear struts, pulling propellers, replacing thrust bearings and replacing carburettors and other engine components, in addition to the full range of more routine maintenance

A self-portrait of Charles Bond in his Tomahawk 'on an air patrol over Rangoon, Burma, in February 1942 at 18,000 ft'. Bond notes that he was bored, so he 'levelled the aircraft and trimmed it for straight and level flying, then held the camera out in front of me at arm's length. I have on helmet, sun glasses and oxygen mask'. Note also the hinged side canopy panel (to the right), used for emergency exits when the canopy could not be slid back (*Charles R Bond, Jr*)

This view of the AVG's improvised Engineering area at Mingaladon gives a good idea of the kind of repair work that had to be done under incredibly primitive conditions. Aircraft numbers have been censored on the negative. While major airframe and engine rebuilding work was generally done by Group Engineering detachments at Toungoo and Kunming, or at CAMCO facilities at Loiwing, much heavy repair work had to be done 'in the field' by the crew chiefs (*Copyright George Rodger*)

Armourers Lee Hanley and Jim Musick service the guns of a Tomahawk at Mingaladon in late January 1942 (*Copyright George Rodger*)

This shot of Chinese crewmen working on Tomahawk '70' provides a good idea of the structural integrity of the Curtiss fighter, and the suitability of its modular airframe for the kind of component swapping that was necessary to keep the AVG in action (*Copyright George Rodger*)

Using a convenient tree as a scaffold, Burmese labourers prepare to hoist the shot-up fuselage of Tomahawk '41' off a CAMCO truck at Mingaladon in late January 1942 (*Copyright George Rodger*)

work. Jacks were available for the aeroplanes, and winches were sometimes rigged in a convenient tree. Generally, tools were not a problem.

Many aeroplanes damaged in ground loops or belly landings could be repaired by cannibalising other wrecks and replacing the propeller, oil cooler and radiators, lower cowling panels, and maybe a wing tip or landing gear strut. But if a crew chief's aeroplane were wrecked beyond what could be repaired overnight, he would be assigned another from the Engineering Section, where even bigger 'rehabilitation' jobs were done involving airframe and engine swaps.

Group Engineering facilities were located at Toungoo and Kunming, with recently-arrived Gerhard Neumann providing invaluable help. CAMCO had similar facilities at Loiwing. Depending on personnel

A Chinese groundcrewman works on the damaged skin of a wing undersurface at Mingaladon in late January 1942. The complex Nationalist Chinese insignia was applied with the aid of a stencil (*Copyright George Rodger*)

The 'Number 10 Factory' at Kunming in late 1942. Although this photo was taken a few months after the AVG had disbanded, it gives a good impression of the conditions under which Group Engineering personnel worked there to 'rehabilitate' wrecked aircraft. Note the mix of aeroplane types, including a P-43 Lancer in the left foreground (*Don Hyatt via Carl Molesworth*)

Third Squadron ground personnel pose in front of Squadron Leader Arvid Olson's Tomahawk '99' at Wu Chia Ba airfield, Kunming, in February 1942. Standing, from left to right, Crew Chief Harold Osborne, Crew Chief Edward Gallagher, Armorer Keith Christensen, Armorer Joseph Poshefko, Crew Chief Glen Blaylock, Crew Chief Leon Colquette, Crew Chief Frank Van Timmeran, Crew Chief Leo Schramm, Crew Chief Henry Olson, Crew Chief Jesse Crookshanks, Crew Chief Wilfred Seiple and Crew Chief John Fauth. In the front row, from left to right, Communications man Charles Francisco, Armorer Paul Perry, Administrative Clerk Daniel Hoyle, Crew Chief Edward Stiles, Armorer Chuck Baisden, Crew Chief Robert A Smith, Communications man Elton Loomis, Crew Chief Charles Engel, Crew Chief Stanley Regis, Operations Clerk Leo Clouthier, Crew Chief Frank Losonsky and Armorer Clarence Riffer. Not present were Communications man Joseph Sweeney, Crew Chief Daniel Keller, Crew Chief George Kepka, Crew Chief Irving Stolet and Communications Clerk Julian Terry. Note the flying jackets for the chilly Kunming weather – a big change from Burma (*Frank Losonsky*)

needs, different crew chiefs were rotated through Engineering. Irving Stolet, who before joining the AVG was an Air Corps welding specialist in the Engineering Section at Mitchell Field, recalls that his first job in Toungoo was to work in Group Engineering, rebuilding 'cracked up' aeroplanes. He did that for six weeks. According to Crew Chief Frank Andersen, only Group Engineering would have kept any records of the airframe and engine changes they made. No records were made of any of the many repairs made on the flightlines.

Andersen recalls that they had a lot of problems with propeller power units and voltage regulators, probably due to the heat and humidity. Since they had no spare parts, there was a constant shortage of props and power units. Some of the ground personnel had no experience with the Curtiss electric propeller, and damaged the electrical contacts before they could be taught proper procedures for pulling the prop. Anderson remembers replacing landing gear and engine parts too. But overall, considering the harsh conditions, Andersen believes the Tomahawk held up well in service.

He recalls a propeller once being hit by a 0.50-cal round when the guns were being sighted. Regulations required that the prop be replaced, but they simply did not have any replacements. So they just pulled out the round and filed off the bulge on the front of the blade. They put it back on and ran up the engine. The vibration was tolerable, so they used it as it was. It was 'kind of scary at times', but they did what they had to do to keep the aeroplanes in service.

Andersen also remembers repairing a lot of battle damage with fabric tape. The procedure was to peen the holes with a hammer, bending in the sharp edges, sand down the area, then dope on strips of aircraft fabric. He recalls doing such a repair on the rudder of Bob Neale's aeroplane, and Neale himself recalled years later how his aeroplane was patched up in this fashion. Frank Losonsky did similar repairs to a shot-up elevator. 'Took a piece of two-inch wide fabric tape. Cut a piece about two inches long, then tucked the fabric under the leading edge of the stabiliser and pulled

Third Squadron pilot Fred S 'Fearless Freddie' Hodges stands next to Tomahawk '83' (P-8183) probably at Kunming in early 1942. Hodges got his nickname for his exaggerated fear of the bugs at Toungoo during training. He participated in most of the Third Squadron's operations, but his only official victory was the destruction of a Ki-43 near Loiwing in April 1942. As the simpler shark head on this aeroplane demonstrates, not all Third Squadron fighters had more intricate artwork (*Chuck Baisden*)

In late January 1942 Chiang Kai-shek demanded that Chennault give Tomahawk flight training to some of his Air Force cadets. These Chinese pilots successfully checked out, and overall they were not much harder on the aeroplanes than the AVG trainees had been. Behind them is Tomahawk '42' (P-8110), which was one of the few AVG Tomahawks painted by Curtiss in the 'mirror image' camouflage pattern (*R T Smith via Brad Smith*)

This was the single casualty of the Chinese cadets' training, Tomahawk '6' (P-8187). This wreck was a perfect candidate for the 'rehabilitation' work for which AVG crewmen were famous. Note that this shark has both a rear view mirror and what appears to be a shoulder harness installation (*R T Smith via Brad Smith*)

it tight over the upper part of the elevator. Next I doped the fabric. The hot climate quickly dried the dope. Two more coats of dope finished the job'.

Joe Poshefko says the rugged P-40 was a terrific aeroplane for the circumstances they were in. He recalls that when the Japanese strafed the aeroplanes at Loiwing, not a single engine was penetrated by their fire. George Bailey remembers problems with rust and mildew on everything. Fuel quality was often suspect and they had problems with fouled spark plugs. They kept the plugs dry in a small box with a burning light bulb.

Bailey and Ed Stiles recall lots of problems with corroded thrust bearings that had to be regularly pulled, cleaned and re-packed.

Nationalist army units were provided as base security detachments in China, and one is seen here marching past parked Third Squadron aircraft at Kunming in the first months of 1942. There were no really effective anti-aircraft guns at any AVG base, however (*R T Smith via Brad Smith*)

According to Frank Losonsky, these problems often resulted in metal particles getting into the engine, and the only fix for this was a complete engine change in Engineering or at Loiwing. But the ground personnel were all very highly qualified, and worked together as a team to solve these never-ending problems. Bailey recalls that some of the men could take apart and put together an Allison engine without the manuals, which was good because all the manuals and technical orders had been lost anyway!

Crew Chief George Tyrell had problems with the backfire screens on the Allison carburettors, in addition to problems with the Curtiss electric propellers. He recalls that they frequently went to the 'junk heap' to get the parts, and sometimes it would take parts from three aeroplanes to get

HARVEY K GREENLAW

John M Williams, Group Communications Officer, Harvey K Greenlaw, Chief of Staff and Group Executive Officer and AVG Commander Claire Chennault await the arrival of a CNAC DC-2 at Kunming in this photo (below), taken in early 1942. Williams worked for Chennault as his communications specialist at the Chinese Air Force flight school at Yunnan-yi before the AVG was formed, and was instrumental in developing the Chinese air raid warning net. When the AVG disbanded, he agreed to induction into the Army Air Forces and continued on

Chennault's staff. Greenlaw, a West Point graduate, had been a CAF flight instructor, then a sales agent representing various US aircraft manufacturers doing business with the Nationalist Chinese, when Chennault offered him the AVG Executive Officer position. As it turned out, most AVG operational work was done by the squadron and flight leaders, and many AVG members wondered what work Greenlaw actually did. In late April Chennault sent him to supervise the destruction of the Loiwing base before it was captured, but apparently he didn't do a very good job of it. Days later he was sent to Delhi to act as liaison with Ferry Command and the Tenth Air Force. He didn't accomplish much there either, and he never returned to China, or any other service in the war effort. His younger wife, Olga, whom Chennault hired to maintain the AVG War Diary, figures more in the story of the group than he does. She recounted her experiences in her memoir *The Lady And The Tigers*. (*Photo Copyright R T Smith via Brad Smith*)

one serviceable. Third Squadron Crew Chiefs Irving Stolet and Edward Stiles remember doing the same.

Obviously little time was available to attend to the appearance of the aircraft, or to keep records of all the mixed airframe components. This is quite apparent when examining photos of AVG aircraft taken at different periods. Some markings faded almost right away. Refreshing red markings was one of the reasons for repainting Third Squadron aircraft in Kunming in January 1942. The brown camouflage paint also faded on the wings and uppersurfaces of the fuselage, while areas not so exposed remained darker. The dark green camouflage paint faded much less. R T Smith remembered it as turning more bluish with time, but this could have been the subjective impression created by the fading brown.

Fuel stains on the left fuselage were heavy, and grime reached remarkable proportions on some aeroplanes. Hasty touch-ups with dark green, sandy brown and very light grey paints can be seen in many photos. Groundcrews in China simply never had the time and materials to devote to 'spit and polish' for aircraft at any stage during the war, and certainly not during the AVG's service.

George Bailey recalls that late in the war, when he was Group Maintenance Officer for the 23rd Fighter Group at Kunming, Gen Clayton Bissell – who had been the bane of Chennault and the AVG – arrived for an inspection tour. Bailey went with Bruce Holloway and Robert Scott to greet him at the airfield. Bissell's first words were 'When in hell are you going to clean up and polish these aeroplanes?' Without thinking, Bailey replied, 'General, I was hoping we could do it the day after the war'. Bailey recalls that they never did get around to cleaning and polishing, and besides, the aeroplanes flew just as well with the grease, oil and dirt on them, and were not as easy to see either.

After Rangoon was evacuated near the end of February, Allied air operations were moved northward to the small British field at Magwe. The Third Squadron had been in reserve status at Kunming since the beginning of January, and had been restored to a strength of 15 aircraft. Chennault started deploying elements of the 'Hell's Angels' to Magwe on 24 February. But the continuing attrition forced Chennault to mix aircraft and personnel from the three squadrons, and ultimately

Greenlaw, Chennault and Williams stand by as the DC-2 is unloaded. The payload consisted of passengers, baggage, mail and various small freight items (*R T Smith via Brad Smith*)

Kunming's 'Main Street' and shopping district as seen through the camera of R T Smith in early 1942 (*R T Smith via Brad Smith*)

AVG 'tourists' draw a crowd of curious Kunming residents in early 1942. Sightseeing was a popular pastime for the 'sights' as well as the 'seers' (*R T Smith via Brad Smith*)

Americans had few opportunities at home to see grain being threshed by hand as it was here near Kunming (*R T Smith via Brad Smith*)

all three had pilots and aeroplanes in action in northern Burma.

The field at Magwe was crude, and still outside the relative safety of the Chinese warning net. The only radar available – the British unit moved from Rangoon – covered only the southern approaches. This left Allied forces vulnerable to surprise attack from Japanese airfields to the east. And the combat odds continued to worsen as the Japanese increased their strength to well over 200 combat aircraft to face about a dozen No 17 Sqn Hurricanes, less than ten AVG Tomahawks and a handful of RAF Blenheims and Lysanders.

Despite some remarkably successful missions from Magwe, the AVG and Commonwealth forces suffered severe losses in air attacks. Ken Jernstedt recalls taking off amidst falling bombs, and no one who served there can forget such experiences. Third Squadron Crew Chief Edward Stiles recalls two occasions when the field was attacked three times each day, destroying most of the accumulated British aircraft and several of the AVG aeroplanes that had not been flown off.

Jernstedt's Tomahawk '88' is seen on the flightline at Wu Chia Ba in early 1942. Note the groundcrew's servicing trucks (*R T Smith via Brad Smith*)

Tomahawk '69' (P-8115) is seen on the flightline at Wu Chia Ba in early 1942. Note that the wheel covers have been reversed. This aeroplane was lost a few weeks later near Chiang Mai, in Thailand (*R T Smith via Brad Smith*)

AVG groundcrewmen used trucks to speed up their servicing operations – in addition to trucks with fuel and oil, one truck was loaded with ammunition, one with oxygen and one with tools and maintenance equipment. The trucks would be rushed to aeroplanes needing service, and rushed away just as quickly when the enemy attacked.

Third Squadron Armorers Keith Christensen and P J Perry were handling the ammunition truck when the field was attacked on 22 March. Christensen sped off and found cover under the trees. He heard the 'all clear' and was almost back on the field when Japanese fighters swooped down and began strafing and dropping anti-personnel bombs. Perry promptly bailed out. Christensen turned the truck around and raced away under fire with the entire supply of ammunition – this was the closest he came to being killed while in the AVG.

Irving Stolet, sent to Magwe after his adventurous trip to Kunming, was meanwhile working on an aeroplane as the bombs fell. Jumping off the wing, he broke an ankle and crawled a hundred yards across the airstrip as the Japanese fighters beat up the field. He wasn't hit, but pilot Frank Swartz and Crew Chief John Fauth were not so lucky, and both later died of their wounds. The next day Chennault ordered his forces to evacuate the field.

The AVG's forward base was now moved back just inside the Chinese border to the CAMCO field at Loiwing. The facilities were better, but the base was still vulnerable to surprise attack. There, the AVG forces – a mix of aircraft and personnel from all three squadrons – would continue to enjoy great success in aerial combat, while the base itself was subjected to unrelenting air attacks. Salvageable Tomahawks and Allison engines had been accumulating there for overhaul too, but little was accomplished on this equipment, much to the disgust of AVG ground personnel who faulted CAMCO management for the lack of support. When Loiwing was captured by the Japanese at the beginning of May, 22 airframes and an undetermined number of engines were still there.

With the southern end of the Burma Road now firmly in its grasp, the objective of the Imperial Army Air Force was now simply to mop up Allied airpower with fighter sweeps and airfield attacks. Commonwealth air forces were virtually destroyed by April, and it is likely that the AVG had no more than 25 to 30 fighters in commission by then. But Japanese losses continued to be high, with the crack 64th Sentai suffering particularly heavy and unexpected losses of experienced pilots.

One of these 64th Sentai pilots was Yohei Hinoki, the 'master falcon'. In typical understatement, he recalled years later for TV cameras that his unit

This scene, captured on film during Second Squadron Crew Chief George Tyrrell's honeymoon drive in March 1942, gives some idea of the kind of adventure that travel on the Burma Road presented (*George Tyrrell*)

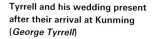

Tyrrell and his wedding present after their arrival at Kunming (*George Tyrrell*)

Robert T Smith's Tomahawk '77' (P-8173) was one of the casualties in the hard-pressed operations at Magwe, being written off due to a crash-landing from engine failure on 23 February 1942. Armorer Keith Christensen is seen here removing the fuselage guns (*Chuck Baisden*)

Tomahawk '38' was left peppered with holes following a near miss by a Japanese fragmentation bomb at Magwe in March 1942 (*Chuck Baisden*)

'had difficulty' fighting against the AVG and 'took a lot of damage'. He remembered that 'their bullets came without stopping, like water pouring from a watering can. There was no way to avoid their bullets. That was the first time I fought against the Americans, and I learned they were tough'. Hinoki spoke with authority – he spent many months recuperating from wounds received in action against the AVG near Loiwing on 10 April 1942.

SHARKS BECOME TIGERS

On 13 March 1942, Charles Bond wrote in his diary that he went to the main barracks to pick up the new 'flying tiger' insignia designed by Walt Disney. 'The emblem is a tiger with all legs outstretched as though in flight,' he wrote, 'leaping out of the angle of a blue V-for-victory'.

These insignia were designed by Roy Williams and Henry Porter of Walt Disney Studios at the request of China Defense Supplies in October 1941, two months before the term 'Flying Tigers' was even in use by the press. But when these decals (and similar enamel pins) were delivered to Kunming, some AVG personnel were less than thrilled by the nickname and the cute tiger emblem. Some probably wondered how the idea of a 'flying tiger' related to their shark-headed

Third Squadron pilots pose for R T Smith's camera outside their quarters at Hostel No 1, in Kunming, in early 1942. They are, from left to right, Paul J. Greene, Tom Haywood, C H 'Link' Laughlin, Robert 'Catfish' Raine, Ken Jernstedt and Chuck Older. These quarters (formerly a school dormitory) were probably the best the AVG ever had (*R T Smith via Brad Smith*)

aeroplanes. But because of the press of operations and the widely scattered airfields at which the aeroplanes were deployed, the decals could not be placed on all the aircraft in service anyway.

The tiger decals were produced in left and right side versions, for placement on each side of the fuselage, and of course they were all identical. They were comprised of two parts – the tiger itself and the large, light blue 'V-for-Victory' segment that the tiger was supposed to be jumping out of. This latter part was seldom used.

It should be noted that these were *not* 'water slide' decals, but high quality 'stick-on' decals – a type that had been in use for aircraft markings for some time. A thin paper sheet protected the top and bottom of each decal. First the bottom sheet was peeled off and the sticky decal was applied to the surface and smoothed down. Then the top sheet was peeled off.

Given the rapid weathering of the aircraft, AVG crewmen often repainted parts of the airframes to make a clean surface when adding new markings. By the time the decals arrived, of course this was more necessary than ever, particularly since they were typically placed just below the rear-view windows – the area most affected by fuel spillage on the port side. Clear dope was also sometimes brushed over them. On some Tomahawks, placement of the tiger decals conflicted with the existing markings. Some photos show that at least a few decals were placed under the cockpit, but then removed in whole (Tomahawk '7') or in part (number '49'), with new ones placed in the 'correct' location further back.

Continuous operations took a heavy toll on men and aircraft, and by March the aeroplanes increasingly were composites rebuilt from parts of several others. Lower cowling panels – where the shark mouths were painted – were particularly vulnerable to damage in crash landings, and so 'first generation' markings were frequently touched up or replaced. But there was now little time or interest in the kind of artistic expression seen before combat started. The work thus tended to be hasty, and the results were usually simpler and cruder than before.

REINFORCEMENTS ARRIVE

But Chennault had finally managed to pry some replacement aircraft from the grasp of the Army, and on 22 March 1942 the first flight of P-40Es arrived in Kunming after a gruelling ferry flight from Accra, in West Africa. Their US insignia and markings were left intact during the ferrying trip, and as far as can be determined, every AVG Kittyhawk was finished in the then-standard Army Air Forces Dark Olive Drab 41 and Neutral Grey 43 camouflage.

After arrival, AVG personnel painted out the fuselage star insignia with dark green paint, and applied Chinese insignia in four positions on the wings directly over the US stars. Most, if not all, of these Chinese insignia were now *decals*, although their blue colour was similar to the royal blue paint already in use for this purpose. Interestingly, and somewhat ironically given the difficult relations between the AVG and the Army Air Forces, the underside *U.S. ARMY* designators were left undisturbed.

Shark heads were promptly added to these aeroplanes, but like virtually all other late vintage AVG paint work, these markings were usually simpler and more hastily applied than those created months before. Each new aeroplane also received a large fuselage number, and many were decorated

Third Squadron Crew Chief Stan Regis relaxes on the wing of a Tomahawk. Regis was a merchant seaman before joining the AVG as a crew chief. Frank Losonsky recalls that Regis was an electrical specialist, and often worked in the Engineering Section, giving him more time to do things like squadron artwork. He also helped lead the salvage operation for the five Tomahawks of Boyington's escort flight that crash-landed in the mountains in early March 1942, and in his spare time he apparently also indulged in some highly dangerous smuggling activity!
(*Frank Losonsky*)

Third Squadron Crew Chief Gail E McCallister poses next to well-worn Tomahawk '49' in May-June 1942. McCallister had a memorable adventure fleeing the Japanese advance up the Burma Road in early May. Delayed by blown bridges on the Salween River, he was often in range of Japanese fire as he walked to Baoshan
(*R T Smith via Brad Smith*)

Third Squadron Flight Leader Robert T Smith shot this photo of some local men and boys posing in front of one of the AVG's new Kittyhawks at Accra, in West Africa, in early March 1942
(*R T Smith via Brad Smith*)

Smith poses by his P-40E Kittyhawk, complete with its water paint 'anti-camouflage' and personal identification markings
(*R T Smith via Brad Smith*)

with the Disney 'Flying Tiger' decals. But not all had squadron bands applied, and none have been documented with any AVG fin serials or squadron markings. And none appear to have had pilot inscriptions or kill markings other than a aeroplane flown by Robert Neale near the end of the AVG's existence.

'Tex' Hill recalls spending considerable time perfecting bombing techniques with these new aeroplanes, and with operations raging virtually non-stop on the China-Burma border, they were quickly put into action by the Second Squadron in ground attack missions.

The Kittyhawks' shark heads of course reflected the different nose contours of that aircraft. They were typically composed of black lips (usually thinner than on the Tomahawks), white teeth (usually smaller and more numerous than before), and a red tongue (now usually larger

AVG crewmen clamber aboard P-40E '107' probably at Kunming in March-April 1942. The simplified markings on this aeroplane were the AVG norm by that date for both these replacement aircraft and for touched up Tomahawks as well
(*R T Smith via Brad Smith*)

This shot of Tomahawk '84' approaching for landing provides a good view of the countryside around the airfield at Kunming in early 1942
(*R T Smith via Brad Smith*)

than before). Initially, the space between the tongue and the upper row of teeth was left Olive Drab. But as time went on, it became popular to fill in this area with black paint.

The shark eyes were usually more pointed than those on the AVG's Tomahawks, although only simple black and/or red pupils can be seen in photos. The fuselage identification numbers on these aircraft were applied sequentially upon receipt in the usual location, but they were generally smaller – and cruder – than those that applied to the Tomahawks. Numbers between '101' and '134' can be seen in photos.

As these new aircraft arrived, many Second Squadron Tomahawks were reallocated to the Third Squadron. No one was now bothering to change the fuselage numbers any more to conform to the initial squadron number blocks, however, although transferred aircraft were repainted with at least new fuselage bands. A few of the Third Squadron's 'new' fighters got 'Hell's Angels' insignia, and many also received the distinctive tricolour pinwheels. In a few cases the re-marking was even more complete. For example, Tomahawk '47' was assigned to Robert T Smith in early May 1942, and he completely updated its markings – those on aircraft '36' and '49' were also significantly updated.

Until the P-40E models arrived, the AVG did not have a truly effective ground attack capability, for the Tomahawks could not carry external ordnance. Chuck Baisden did, however, rig a Tomahawk to drop small stick-type incendiaries from its flare chutes, and another so it could drop concussion grenades. Both improvisations were used in the successful 18 March 1942 attack on Japanese air bases at Mudon and Moulmein, in Burma, although only the incendiaries worked properly. According to Baisden, Group Headquarters Armorers Roy Hoffman and Harvey Wirta also fabricated a rack under the fuselage of a Tomahawk that would carry a bomb, but they couldn't get it to work properly.

On the other hand, the new P-40Es could carry a belly tank or a bomb under the fuselage, or six small bombs on wing racks – the more usual load. AVG armourers

Group photographers Jim Regis (left) and Joseph H Pietsker look for some photo ops on the flightline at Kunming in early 1942 (*R T Smith via Brad Smith*)

Group Operations and Supply Officer C B 'Skip' Adair emerges from his 1941 Plymouth staff car at Kunming in early 1942. Adair had worked with Chennault in China for several years, running the Chinese Air Force primary training facility at Yunnan-yi. In 1940 he returned to the USA and recruited Army personnel for the AVG, and then agreed to join Chennault's staff, primarily as supply officer. Adair later served as Executive Officer when Harvey Greenlaw was absent, and after the AVG disbanded, he was inducted in China into the Army Air Forces (*R T Smith via Brad Smith*)

An AVG jeep rolls down the flightline at Kunming in the Spring of 1942. Note Tomahawk '81' in the background (*R T Smith via Brad Smith*)

A Chinese helper takes a break at Kunming in May or June 1942. Note the servicing truck and basketball goal in the background (*R T Smith via Brad Smith*)

T C Haywood's Tomahawk '49' is 'gassed up' from a fuel truck on the flightline prior to a mission. This was sophisticated and rare equipment by AVG standards (*Frank Losonsky*)

Tomahawk '49' again, this time with Third Squadron Flight Leader Thomas C Haywood posing on the wing of his 'new' fighter, at Kunming in May-June 1942. Note his personal horned bulldog insignia, which was carried on both sides, and the remains of a Disney tiger decal under the cockpit. The wing root stencilling is also visible in this shot. Haywood flew in the Third Squadron's first combat over Rangoon on 23 December 1941. The first to spot the approaching Japanese bombers, he blurted out 'Hey Mac, I see the bastards!' He claimed the destruction of one Ki-21 in this engagement, but was hit by the escorts and forced to withdraw. Haywood was credited with two more 'Sallys' in the famous Christmas Day air battle, and had an official total of 5.08 victories. After the AVG, he worked as a test pilot for Consolidated-Vultee, and later flew for the Flying Tiger Line (*R T Smith via Brad Smith*)

recall that they obtained ordnance from the Chinese, who had stored it for long periods in graveyards, caves and warehouses. The largest bombs were of Soviet manufacture, and weighed about 250 kg. They had only one carrying lug, however, so a band with another lug was fabricated so they could be hung from the Kittyhawks' belly shackles.

The AVG was also offered the use of smaller fragmentation, anti-personnel and incendiary bombs of probable Chinese or French manufacture. This was the most-used ordnance, even though AVG armourers refused to have anything to do with much of it. Chuck Baisden recalls that some French anti-personnel bombs of Great War vintage were especially questionable.

No one can know for sure, but it is possible that two AVG pilots lost their lives due to prematurely detonating bombs. Third Squadron Armorer Joe Poshefko recalls being asked one day by Chennault if he could read Russian, because the Chinese had some Soviet time-delay bombs on hand. These were designed as aerial weapons that would detonate among enemy bomber formations. Poshefko couldn't read Russian, and after seeing these old and delicate weapons, decided that he didn't want to touch them. A Chinese pilot volunteered to test one however. The bomb blew up as he was taxiing, and 'that was the end of that idea'.

Poshefko also recalls some experiments with improvised incendiaries using belly tanks with gasoline and 0.50-cal rounds as detonators, but they never worked. A few American-made bombs finally began to arrive just before the AVG disbanded, too late to be of much use.

By the middle of April 1942, the Allied front in Burma had totally collapsed. Chiang Kai-shek was increasingly demanding that Chennault,

now commissioned in the Army Air Forces, send his pilots on low-level 'morale missions' so the beleaguered troops in northern Burma could see for themselves that a Chinese Air Force was still supporting them. But not only was such top-down mission planning alien to the AVG way of doing things, the missions offered no benefit for the high risks involved. Third Squadron pilot Charles Older remembered years later that;

'They wanted us to go down there and fly around at low altitudes, just sort of motor around casually to let the Chinese see the insignia on our aeroplanes to boost their morale. Well, my thinking was that their morale wouldn't be boosted very much by seeing us get shot down doing that kind of silly nonsense, and so why do it?'

On 22 April the unrest boiled over into a threatened strike – what Chennault later referred to as the 'pilots' revolt'. Over 20 pilots threatened to resign if these missions were not discontinued, and after a heated meeting, the matter was forgotten and no more of these operations were ordered. But in Ken Jernstedt's opinion, most post-war writers have blown this matter out of proportion. He recalls that tempers got much hotter a few weeks later when the Army clumsily tried to induct the AVG. But the war was going bad enough without the unnecessary danger of these missions, and on 29 April AVG forces had to evacuate Loiwing and move operations further north to Baoshan and Yunnan-yi.

Although Japanese raids continued, the protective umbrella of the Chinese early warning system now covered AVG bases better. Nonetheless, attrition from all causes was high as equipment wore out. By early May Japanese forces were nearing the Chinese border at the Salween River Gorge, and the AVG's meagre forces were pressed into the bombing role with the antiquated ordnance provided by the Nationalist Chinese.

In a series of sharp attacks from 6 to 9 May, AVG 'bombers' inflicted heavy losses on Japanese ground forces. The Chinese army had meanwhile destroyed several miles of the Burma Road and its bridges, and with the Monsoon season underway again, the Japanese advance came to an end. The Burma Road, however, was closed.

Although air activity was increasingly sporadic in China in the weeks following these climactic ground attacks, during that period Chennault conducted perhaps some of his most innovative and resourceful operations of the war. On 12 May AVG forces escorted a surprise attack on

Third Squadron Armorer Clarence W Riffer (left) and Line Chief Frank Van Timmeran lean on the stabiliser of Tomahawk '49' at Kunming in May-June 1942. Many AVG men worried about gaining weight during the long cruise to Burma. As the photos in this book attest, this was obviously not a problem once they were overseas!
(*R T Smith via Brad Smith*)

Tomahawk '47' (P-8127) was originally the assigned aircraft of Second Squadron Flight Leader John Petach, but it was transferred to the Third Squadron and allocated to Robert T Smith in May 1942. Smith thoroughly cleaned it and updated its markings, and this was the result. Note that even this meticulously repainted aeroplane features the now-standard simpler style of shark head
(*R T Smith via Brad Smith*)

Tomahawk '36' was originally the assigned aircraft of Ed Rector of the Second Squadron, but it was also transferred to the Third Squadron in April-May 1942, with whom it is show serving in this photo. Note the characteristic Third Squadron pinwheels. By this time its blue shark 'lips' had also been updated with black (*Frank Losonsky*)

Japanese installations at Hanoi. Chennault then staged a decoy force northward to Chongqing on 5 June. Next, making effective use of dummy aircraft to fool Japanese reconnaissance, he quickly re-deployed this force to bases in south-east China at Hengyang, Lingling and Guilin for operations against installations on the coast.

Some of the AVG's most success-ful air combats took place during these operations. Satoshi Anabuki, the Imperial Army's leading wartime ace, told documentary filmmakers years later that 'Gen Chennault and his American unit based in China were tough opponents. He organised battle very well, so we had to be on guard against his attacks'.

OUT OF SERVICE, INTO LEGEND

It was decided that the AVG would be officially decommissioned on 4 July 1942, and as this date approached Brig Gen Clayton Bissell and the Army Air Forces made heavy-handed and insulting attempts to get all the 'Flying Tigers' to accept immediate induction in China. There were 87 pilots and 164 ground personnel remaining on its roster. Of these, five pilots and 34 crewmen agreed to accept immedi-ate induction into the USAAF in China, and 19 pilots and 24 groundcrewmen extended their CAMCO contracts by two-week so as to help smooth the transition. Two of pilots were killed in action, and on 9 July Peter Wright shot down the last Japanese aeroplane claimed by a member of the AVG.

Close-up of Tomahawk '36' – the number is barely visible above the eye. Note the ever-present servicing truck in the background. This photo was again taken at Kunming, probably in May 1942 (*R T Smith via Brad Smith*)

A line-up of Third Squadron aircraft, probably at Kunming in the Spring of 1942. Note that two of the three aeroplanes sport the simpler shark head designs that became the norm as the time for intricate artwork vanished (*Frank Losonsky*)

83

Army personnel had been trickling into the theatre for months, and on 3 July 1942, the USAAF's 16th FS reached Kunming with 16 P-40Es and 22 pilots to supplement the assets to be turned over by the AVG. These consisted of 28 Tomahawks, of which 18 were serviceable, and 18 Kittyhawks, of which 17 were serviceable. Ten P-43s were also borrowed from the Nationalist Chinese Air Force, although these were of limited usefulness due to fuel tanks that tended to leak into the supercharger air ducting.

The 23rd FG of the China Air Task Force (CATF) replaced the AVG – the CATF was reorganised as the Fourteenth Air Force in March 1943. On its first day of operations it had 51 serviceable aircraft and 24 pilots. Its first group and squadron commanders were all AVG veterans.

Eleven AVG pilots had been killed in action or died of combat wounds, nine died in accidents and one AVG groundcrewman died of wounds sustained in an enemy air attack. Three AVG pilots had been captured, and two went missing (and undoubtedly lost their lives). As near as can be determined, AVG aircraft losses were more or less as follows – 12 in aerial combat, 12 to ground fire, 10 (this figure includes two Kittyhawks lost to ground fire on 10 July 1942 while on the rolls of the 23rd FG, and it would appear that 8-10 other Kittyhawks are not accounted for), 13 in air raids, 23 written off in accidents and 22 left behind in the Loiwing evacuation.

With their AVG markings still in place, and US star insignia hastily painted over the Chinese sun with Nationalist Chinese royal blue paint, the AVG's surviving fighters soldiered on with their new owners. The Tomahawks remained in service in China until early 1943, although largely in reserve roles. The few remaining aeroplanes were then ferried to India, where they finished their days in an operational training unit. Some of the P-40Es lasted a while longer.

The AVG Disney tiger decals, often with a few painted-on additions signifying America jumping into the battle in China, became for a while the emblem of the 23rd FG, and the men of Chennault's later command avidly accepted the nickname of 'Flying Tigers' as well. And all of their P-40s would wear the shark head motif inherited from the AVG.

Thirty-three AVG personnel received the Nationalist Chinese Order of the Cloud Banner, and many AVG pilots received the Nationalist Chinese Air Force Medal. After their AVG service, 16 pilots flew for China National Airways Corporation, and a number of others took test pilot and airline jobs. Some 25 ex-AVG pilots and 105 groundcrewmen returned to military service, and of these, 14 were subsequently killed in action during the war.

Thirteen former AVG groundcrewmen completed flight training. Gil Bright became one of the first American pilots to be credited with shooting down Japanese, German and Italian aircraft, and James Howard and 'Pappy' Boyington received the Medal of Honor for their service later in the war. But while China and Britain decorated several AVG members, for over 50 years the United States did not recognise the AVG as a US military organisation. Finally, on 8 December 1996, all the honourably discharged flying personnel of the AVG were belatedly awarded the Distinguished Flying Cross, and all honourably discharged ground personnel the Bronze Star.

Ex-AVG Tomahawks of the 74th FS are seen at Kunming in the Autumn of 1942, the three machines closest to the camera featuring updated Disney 'flying tiger' insignia. Since airframe rebuilding and cannibalising was a never-ending process, the side numbers worn by these machines may not necessarily have been those used by the fighters during their AVG service (*Leon Klesman via Carl Molesworth*)

The wreckage of Tomahawk '69' is now on display at the Thai Air Force Base at Chiang Mai, the airfield it had attacked so many years ago. An Allison engine fitted in Tomahawk '47' has also recently been unveiled at the Tomahawk Project at the Torrance, California Airport. How it survived and got to the United States is a mystery. These are the only known AVG Tomahawk relics in existence today, although other examples of the Curtiss fighter have recently been recovered from the former Soviet Union and, amazingly, these were all from the same production series as the AVG's aeroplanes.

AVG pilots were officially credited with the destruction of 296 aircraft in the air and on the ground. Twenty-six pilots were credited by CAMCO with the destruction of five or more aircraft – eighteen of them with five or more aerial victories. There is no way of knowing how absolutely accurate such figures are, although it is widely accepted by historians that *all* such numbers throughout the history of air warfare have tended to be inflated to one degree or another for very understandable reasons. But by any measure, the accomplishments of the ragged American Volunteer Group were extraordinary.

The AVG was undermanned and incompletely trained, and equipped with what were considered obsolete aircraft. The spare parts necessary to maintain serviceability were not available. Radio equipment was poor, and its improvised optical gunsights were unreliable. There were no good maps or direction-finding equipment, and in that part of the world even the simplest cross-country flight was hazardous in such short-range aeroplanes.

Groundcrews usually worked in the open with limited tools and equipment, and often had to use fuel of doubtful quality. The food and living quarters were usually dismal. Diseases and unsanitary water put most AVG members out of action for long periods, and for months the group operated outside the protection of a reliable early warning network.

YUNNAN WHORE, photographed at Kunming some time in 1942 following the AVG disbandment, provides an example of how the 23rd FG added its own personal markings to ex-AVG aircraft. Note the heavily dented cowling, the hasty quality of the shark head and the generally 'beaten-up' appearance of this veteran. USAAF data stencils were added to some H81-A-2s as well, and these indicate that the Army considered them to be *de facto* P-40Bs (*Leon Klesman via Carl Molesworth*)

Yet at a time when the outcome of the war was far from decided, and Allied forces in the Far East were suffering one demoralising defeat after another, the American Volunteer Group regularly bested a numerically superior enemy and galvanised American spirit and determination. The AVG also had America's first 'nose artists' in that war, and although the motif did not originate with them, the powerful image of their gaudily marked 'sharks of the air' will always symbolise their achievements in that terrible conflict.

APPENDICES

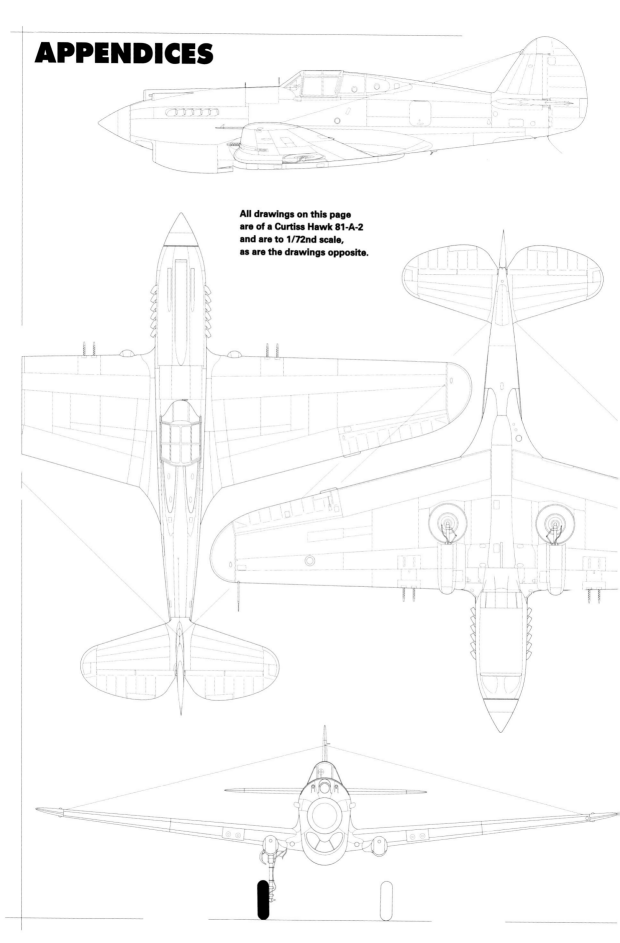

All drawings on this page
are of a Curtiss Hawk 81-A-2
and are to 1/72nd scale,
as are the drawings opposite.

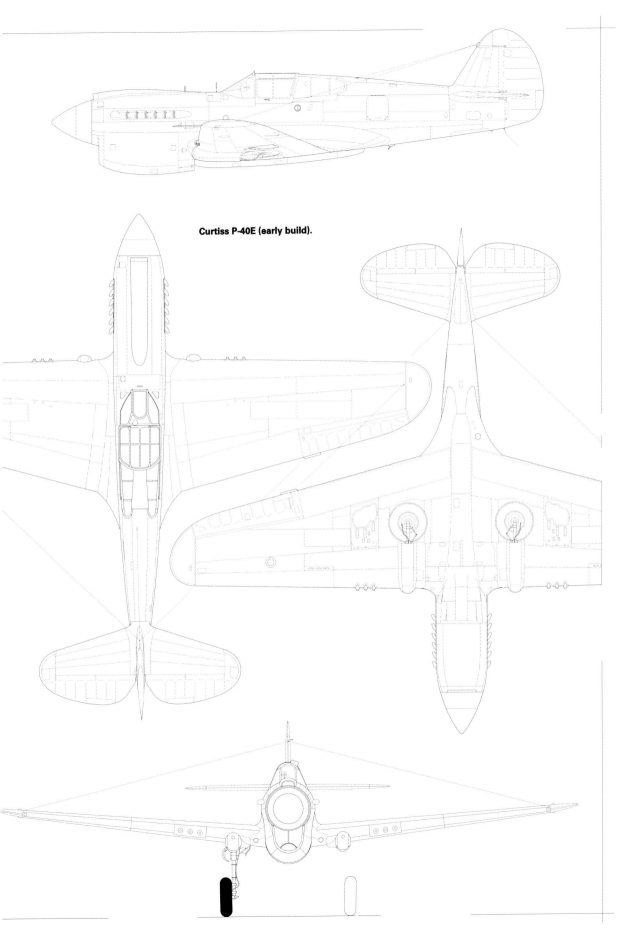

Curtiss P-40E (early build).

COLOUR PLATES

1

Hawk 81-A-2 number '3' (CAF serial number P-8103), assigned to J Richard Rossi of the First Squadron, Rangoon, Burma, February 1942

This was one of a few aeroplanes that never received a shark head, probably because it was in maintenance at the time these were being applied in November-December 1941. It had no squadron insignia either, but it did wear the First Squadron's white fuselage band and personal markings, consisting of small Chinese and American insignia on either side of the fuselage. These were made with the same stencils applied to many AVG ground vehicles. It cannot be determined from the available photos if a pilot ID inscription was carried, although Rossi recalls that his name was on it. Wheel covers were probably Dark Earth. This aeroplane was also flown by William Bartling, among others, and it was written off at Rangoon, probably on 23 February 1942.

Flight Leader John Richard ('Dick') Rossi was a flight instructor at Pensacola Naval Air Station when he signed up with the AVG. He arrived at Rangoon on 12 November 1941 with one of the last contingents of AVG personnel, and thus missed Chennault's training program. His first encounters with the enemy came during battles with 50th and 77th Sentai Ki-27s over Burma on 19 and 28 January 1942 while flying Tomahawks '18' and '5', respectively. Following the second combat Rossi was credited with the destruction of a Ki-27. He was credited with another 'Nate' during an interception mission on 25 February. The next day another flight of 'Lilys' and 'Nates' was intercepted, and Rossi was credited with shooting down three more. Following the retreat out of Burma, he flew Tomahawks '38' and '59'. On 12 June he was credited with the destruction of a Ki-48 'Lily' bomber. After dissolution of the AVG on 4 July 1942, Rossi joined China National Airways Corporation and flew transports over the 'Hump'. He may well hold the all-time record for these dangerous missions, completing at least 738 (some sources say more than 750). After the war he flew for Chennault's clandestine Civil Air Transport (CAT) and Central Aviation Transport Corporation. He joined Flying Tiger Airlines in 1950, and retired in 1973. Rossi was officially credited with 6.29 victories in the AVG.

2

Hawk 81-A-2 number '5' (CAF serial probably P-8198), assigned to First Squadron Vice Leader Charles R Bond, Loiwing, China, April 1942

The shark mouth on this aircraft is a good example of the most common basic AVG style in black, red and white, with the camouflage showing inside the mouth. The eyes were white with black or green pupils and red detailing. Unlike many other aeroplanes, the small nose numbers on '5' was not painted over when the shark mouth was added. This aeroplane carried a representative version of the 'Adam and Eve' insignia, comprised of a light green apple entwined by a black snake, with white stick figures of 'Eve' chasing 'Adam' on the body of the apple. White lettering on the snake read *1st Pursuit* or *First Pursuit*. An inscription in front of the cockpit read *PILOT: BOND/C.C.: DOLAN*. This aeroplane was

put out of action in a strafing attack on Loiwing on 10 April 1942. It may have carried Disney tiger decals and kill markings by that time, although there are no known photos of this. It is believed that the wreckage of this aeroplane was cannibalised for parts for Tomahawk '74'.

3

Hawk 81-A-2 number '7' (CAF serial P-8194), assigned to First Squadron Leader Robert Neale, Kunming, China, June 1942

The available evidence indicates that the identification number '7' was first placed on aeroplane P-8146, then became associated with P-8172 in late January 1942 and finally P-8194 in late March, when parts of those last two airframes were merged. Note evidence of damage to the fin and rudder. The shark mouth was in typical black, white and red colours. The eye had an eccentric black pupil with probable red detailing – a style seen on several First Squadron aircraft. The 'Adam and Eve' insignia on this aeroplane was in an elaborate 'cartoon' style, with a darker than usual shade of green for the apple (see the enlarged view of this insignia on page 59). Wheel covers were in the First Squadron's white colour, which was the only known instance of such a marking. An inscription near the cockpit read *PILOT/R.NEALE*. This aeroplane featured one of the tiger decals designed by the Disney Studios that the AVG received in March 1942 (again see the enlarged view of this insignia on page 58). In fact, it appears that one had earlier been placed under the cockpit, then removed. The identification number on the starboard side was located about 12 inches further forward than the number on the port side – perhaps the result of the complicated history of this airframe. This aircraft survived to serve with the 23rd FG. Neale, of course, also frequently flew other Tomahawks, including numbers '23' and '94', as well as P-40E Kittyhawks beginning in May.

4

Hawk 81-A-2 number '13' (CAF serial P-8102), assigned to James D Cross of the First Squadron, Rangoon, Burma, January 1942

Aircraft '13's' shark mouth was applied in black, white and red like most Tomahawks in the First and Second Squadrons. The eye featured a large black pupil, trimmed in red. The squadron identification band was dirty, or 'toned down' in some fashion to make it less conspicuous – the small nose number was treated the same way. This aeroplane featured a pilot inscription in the usual location – *PILOT/J.D.CROSS*. The First Squadron insignia, which may have been the first one applied by designer Charles Bond, set the pattern for most others, but had no lettering (see the enlarged view of this insignia on page 58). The smaller chalk outline was probably Bond's initial demonstration sketch, with the painted insignia the final result after talking it over with Cross. Wheel covers were light grey. National insignia had been over-painted on both the upper- and undersurfaces of the wings some time prior to those seen here being applied. This aeroplane had a rear-view mirror mounted above the windscreen. Joe Rosbert flew this Tomahawk in the AVG's first combat on 20 December 1941, but according to several entries in Bond's AVG diary, this aircraft was a 'lemon'! It was almost certainly written-off and 'parted-out' to Tomahawk '53' (P-8170) in late February 1942.

James D Cross was serving as an Army Air Corps Ferry Command pilot when he joined the AVG. He arrived at Toungoo on 12 November 1941, and got off to an inauspicious start when on his check flight in Tomahawk '11' his engine blew a rod and caught fire, forcing him to belly-in from 1000 ft. He took part in some of the AVG's earliest scrambles at Toungoo in early December 1941, although he failed to encounter the enemy. Finally, on 20 December he participated in the AVG's first combat mission from Kunming. He was apparently credited with .27 of a victory, which was his total for his AVG service. By mid-January 1942 Charles Bond was describing Cross in his diary as a 'red-ass', or chronic complainer, but a few weeks later his attitude improved when he was promoted to Flight Leader. On 21 February 1942 he was one of six 'Flying Tigers' that fought 77th Sentai 'Nates' and bombers near the Salween River Gorge. Four days later, in a battle with 'Nates' of the 50th and 77th Sentais, and now probably flying Tomahawk number '78', he was wounded in the face and arm by flying glass and fragments from several 7.7 mm rounds. After a trip to India for treatment and rest, he participated in a poorly-conducted operation ferrying P-43 Lancers to China. Apparently, he flew no more after that, and served out his AVG contract as a liaison officer with the Nationalist Chinese Air Force in Chongqing. Following his AVG service, Cross became a pilot for Pan American Airways.

5

Hawk 81-A-2 Number '18' (CAF Serial P-8197), assigned to First Squadron Flight Leader Matt Kuykendall, Rangoon, Burma, January-February 1942,
This aircraft's shark head was in the common pattern in black, white and red. Like some other First Squadron aeroplanes, its eye was more intricate than usual, but in the same colours as the mouth. This fighter did not have a First Squadron insignia, and like a few other First Squadron machines, it had a dirtied or 'off-white' fuselage number. The wheel covers were Dark Earth. This Tomahawk was also regularly flown by Richard Rossi during the Rangoon campaign.

Matthew Kuykendall was an Army pilot stationed at Maxwell Field when he joined the AVG. He was posted to Rangoon with the First Squadron, where he participated in interceptions without being credited with any victories. On 29 January he was shot up over Rangoon, and had a bullet crease his forehead. The ever-colourful newspaper accounts reported that he landed with oil 'squirting all over the cockpit'. Several months later he was fined $100 for firing his sidearm 'in a reckless manner while intoxicated and off duty'. He was downed a Ki-27 on 5 May for his one victory recognised by CAMCO, and he served in the AVG to disbandment.

6

Hawk 81-A-2 number '21' (CAF serial P-8182), assigned to First Squadron Vice Leaders Frank Schiel and Greg 'Pappy' Boyington, Rangoon, Burma, January-February 1942
Tomahawk '21's shark head design was in the popular First and Second Squadron style in black, red and white, with simple red and white eyes. The First Squadron insignia featured white lettering on the snake (probably *1st Pur.*). The fuselage and nose identification numbers were either 'dirtied'

or painted pale grey/off white. No pilot inscription or kill markings were carried. Note the patch of dark green paint on the fuselage between the exhaust stack and the canopy – perhaps a green apple insignia had been placed there in error by a painter influenced by the work already in progress in the Third Squadron.

Ex-Army P-40 pilot Frank Schiel was credited with seven victories in the AVG, the first of these being scored on 24 January when he shot down a 'Nate' over Rangoon. He also frequently flew solo reconnaissance missions, and on 5 May he was credited with the destruction of an 11th Sentai Ki-27. Schiel later flew Kittyhawks on ground attack missions against the advancing Japanese in northern Burma. He was involved in the 12 May raid on the Japanese air base at Hanoi, where he was credited with the destruction of three Japanese aircraft on the ground. By May there were only eight aeroplanes in commission in the Second Squadron for its 20 pilots, and Schiel often led the increasingly numerous ground attack missions in support of Chinese troops on the Salween River front. On 22 June he was credited with the destruction of another 'Nate'. After disbandment of the AVG, he stayed on in China to become the first commander of the 74th FS/23rd FG. He was killed in a flying accident on 5 December 1942 while on a reconnaissance mission in bad weather.

Gregory Boyington was a Marine Corps lieutenant before joining the AVG as a Flight Leader. He was credited with the destruction of a 'Nate' on 29 January 1942, and eight days later he was credited with two more. Bob Neale was appointed Squadron Leader following the death of Robert Sandell in a flying accident on 7 February, and in turn he appointed Boyington Vice Squadron Leader. Boyington's flying and fighting skills were highly regarded at the time, but his increasingly erratic and belligerent off-duty behaviour had rapidly alienated nearly everyone, and Neale soon regretted his decision. On 15 February Boyington reported for duty badly hung over, and got into a nasty argument with Neale, and after that the latter relied on Charles Bond for scheduling and operational planning. Similar problems occurred as the weeks went by, and on 6 March Boyington embarrassed AVG Commander Claire Chennault at an awards ceremony hosted by Madame and Chiang Kai-shek. The next day he was unexpectedly given leadership of an honour guard for the Chiangs when flight leader Frank Lawlor had to abort the mission. Boyington, who had apparently not paid attention to the pre-flight briefing, got off-course and the entire flight ran out of fuel and had to crash-land in the mountains. Boyington later managed to fly out two of the aeroplanes after extensive field repair work by the groundcrews, but the other aeroplanes had to be salvaged. Further conduct problems followed, including fights with Bond and Bill Bartling, although Boyington continued to perform well in combat missions. In April he was injured at Loiwing when he ran Tomahawk '92' off the runway on take-off, then crashed a nearby truck into a tree. Boyington said his engine had lost power, but the aeroplane's crew chief, Leo J Schramm, stated in his memoir that the engine had checked out fine, and the crewmen thought that the pilot had been drinking. Further problems ensued, and within days he quit/was discharged. As he wrote of this period in his famous memoir, *Baa, Baa, Black Sheep*, 'I was an emotionally immature person of the first order, which does not help peace of mind or make happiness. Frankly, this is what makes screwballs, and I'm afraid that I was one'. He was officially credited with 3.5 victories in the AVG, and apparently had one other unrecognised claim. Boyington returned to the Marines and commanded F4U Corsair-equipped VMF-214 – the legendary 'Black Sheep Squadron' – with whom he was scored an 22 additional victories before being shot down on 3 January 1944 and taken prisoner at Rabaul. Unlike virtually all Allied prisoners held there, he survived due to a sympathetic Japanese interpreter arranging for him to be moved to Japan. Boyington was later decorated with the Medal of Honor.

7

Hawk 81-A-2 number '25' (CAF serial P-8144), assigned to Einar 'Mickey' Mickelson of the First Squadron, Rangoon, Burma, January 1942

In addition to the typical shark mouth, this aircraft featured an eye with a black pupil and a thin, oval-shaped red edge around it. The inscription *Pilot: Mickelson* was placed near the cockpit, and the crew chief's name was placed under the serial number on the fin – *Curran* or *Jake* are possibilities. Photos indicate that an 'Adam and Eve' insignia was chalked onto this aeroplane, but may not have been painted. Personal markings consisted of what appears to be an illustration torn from a magazine and doped on just forward of the cockpit. Wheel covers were light grey. This aeroplane was destroyed on one of Rangoon's numerous dispersal fields, probably on 1 February.

Not much seems to be known of Einar Mickelson's career in the AVG, although it would seem that he did not fly this Tomahawk very often. He was credited by CAMCO with .27 of a victory, but appears in various accounts of the AVG more often as a pilot of transport and liaison aircraft. However, Mickelson was still on the roster of the First Squadron during its posting to Rangoon in January and February 1942. On 22 February 1942, just before Rangoon was evacuated, he was sent with two other pilots north to Magwe to provide air cover over the northward route of retreat. It seems that he flew few combat missions after that. Mickelson served until the AVG was disbanded, and after that he joined the China National Airways Corporation and flew transports on the dangerous missions over the 'hump' and throughout China. He was killed in the crash of CNAC flight 75 at Baoshan, China, on 20 February 1944.

8

Hawk 81-A-2 number '33' (CAF serial P-8151), assigned to First Squadron Flight Leader Robert Little, Kunming, China, April 1942

Again, this shark mouth has been painted in the popular black, white and red colours, but with three 'dimples' at the rear and a thin brown edge on top of the tongue. The eye featured a pinkish (or faded red) pupil, with a thin brown edge around the front of the white element. This aeroplane had a pilot inscription in the usual location – *PILOT/R.LITTLE*. Also note the crew chief's name below the fin serial (*Curran*). The 'Adam and Eve' insignia was outlined in white, and the plain black snake wore a black top hat. The insignia had no lettering, however. The wheel covers were painted Dark Earth.

9

Hawk 81-A-2 number '34' (CAF Serial P-8196), assigned to Second Squadron Leader John Newkirk, Toungoo, Burma, December 1941

The shark mouth on this machine was in the most common pattern and colours, with eyes in white and red. A previous fuselage number was painted out before the one seen here was added, probably just before deployment. Photographic evidence is inconclusive regarding whether Bert Christman actually completed his cartoon caricature of the urbane 'Scarsdale Jack' on this aeroplane (see detail painting on page 58).

10

Hawk 81-A-2 number '36' (CAF serial P-8123), assigned to Second Squadron Vice Leader Edward Rector, Rangoon, Burma, January-February 1942

This shark head design was one of several in the Second Squadron that featured blue lips with the red tongue and white teeth. The eye was white and blue (see enlarged view on page 59). An identification number was originally placed under the cockpit, but was painted over with dark green. The fuselage band was in the usual blue identification colour. This aeroplane had no pilot inscription, kill marks, squadron insignia or Disney tiger decals during its Second Squadron service. It was reassigned to the Third Squadron in April-May 1942, where it was repainted with a red fuselage band and red, white and blue pinwheels. The lips and eye of the shark head were also repainted black, and the nose identification number painted out. No 'Hell's Angels' figures were added, however. This aeroplane survived AVG service and, as number '220', was used by the 23rd FG. Note that it had a rear-view mirror.

11

Hawk 81-A-2 number '44' (CAF Serial P-8184), assigned to Second Squadron Flight Leader Peter Wright, Rangoon, Burma, January 1942

This aeroplane featured a blue-lipped shark head with a red 'doughnut' eye. It was wrecked in a tragic landing accident at Mingaladon on the night of 7-8 January 1942 that resulted in the death of Ken Merritt, who was asleep in a parked car near the airstrip.

12

Hawk 81-A-2 number '45' (CAF Serial P-8165), assigned to Percy Bartelt of the Second Squadron, Kunming, China, March 1942

The shark head of this machine was rendered in the more typical black/white/red colour scheme, but the eye featured a red 'doughnut' shape for the pupil. The side number was dirtied or painted an off-white colour, as was the smaller nose number. The underwing insignia were slightly larger than usual, and the aeroplane carried no pilot inscription. This shark head was the second of two designs worn by the machine as a result of extensive repairs after the aeroplane had been 'nosed up' during the squadron's service at Rangoon.

Former Navy pilot Percy Bartelt was one of four Second Squadron pilots who attacked the Japanese airfield at Mae Sot on 8 January 1942, sharing in a victory total of eight aircraft destroyed on the ground. He was also credited with shooting down three Ki-30 light bombers on 23 January and two 'Nates' 24 hours later. Some time after that, Bartelt was transferred to the Third Squadron. Greg Boyington and Bartelt embarrassed Chennault at the 4 March 1942 banquet with the Chiangs, and Bartelt was dismissed/resigned from the AVG on 21 March 1942. He compiled a record of 7.00 victories paid by CAMCO.

13

Hawk 81-A-2 number '47' (CAF serial P-8127), assigned to Second Squadron Flight Leader John Petach, Rangoon, Burma, January-February 1942

This aeroplane also featured a blue-lipped shark mouth and a blue eye. It was one of the few Tomahawks on which Bert Christman completed a pilot caricature – in this case a 'cycling panda', commemorating Petach's cycling prowess (see detail painting on page 58). The colours of the cartoon are unknown, although black and white certainly predominated. No pilot inscription or kill markings were carried on this aircraft during its Second Squadron service. In late May 1942 '47' was transferred to the Third Squadron . . .

14

Hawk 81-A-2 number '47' (CAF serial P-8127), assigned to Robert T Smith of the Third Squadron, Kunming, China, June 1942

. . . where it was assigned to R T Smith. On 4 June its new pilot began cleaning it up and updating the markings, and the end result is seen here in profile. The shark head was refreshed in black, red and white, and the eye was also painted black. The serial and fuselage numbers remained the same as before, but an inscription was added near the cockpit, reading *PILOT/R.T.SMITH*. Smith painted over the nose number, repainted the identification band red and added ten small kill flags. Stan Regis added his 'Hell's Angels' figures, and a Disney tiger decal was also applied after the surface under it had been cleaned and/or repainted. Third Squadron red, blue and white pinwheels completed the markings. Bert Christman's cartoon on the starboard side was not disturbed. This aeroplane survived AVG service and ended its days with the 23rd FG as number '14'.

15

Hawk 81-A-2 number '48' (CAF serial P-8134), assigned to David Lee 'Tex' Hill of the Second Squadron, Toungoo, Burma, December 1941

Although an immensely popular subject for illustrators, few seem to realise that this aeroplane had actually seen no combat up to the point when it was written off as a result of a landing accident following an otherwise uneventful pre-dawn scramble at Toungoo on 9 December 1941. The shark mouth was in black and red. The cowl panel where the shark eye was located had been removed when the reference photo for this illustration was taken following the crash, and the panda 'cowboy' cartoon was obscured by the wing. Thus, placement and exact details of these features are conjectural. It is known that Bert Christman favoured the starboard aft fuselage for his pilot caricatures, and according to 'Tex' Hill, he definitely completed his artwork on '48'. If Christman placed one on the port side of his friend Hill's fighter as well, it certainly would have looked like that illustrated here.

16

Hawk 81-A-2 number '49' (CAF serial P-8133), assigned to Tom Haywood of the Third Squadron, Kunming, China, May-June 1942

This aircraft was originally assigned to Frank Swartz of the Second Squadron. The shark mouth was still in the popular white, black and red scheme that the aeroplane had worn with the 'Panda Bears', but the eye now had a red pupil with a light-coloured centre spot (probably light blue or pink). The fuselage band had been repainted red, and the aeroplane wore a new inscription – *PILOT/T.C.HAYWOOD*. A two-line crew chief inscription was placed opposite it on the starboard side. Wheel covers were light grey. Note that this aeroplane had the light blue 'V' portion of the Disney 'flying tiger' decal applied, and the remains of one of these tigers under the cockpit. It also featured a nicely rendered 'horned bulldog' insignia on both sides of the fuselage just below and forward of the cockpit (see detail view on page 58). The colours of this marking, and the artist who rendered it, remain unknown, although it was certainly applied after the aeroplane was assigned to Haywood. No 'Hell's Angels' were added, but Bert Christman's caricature of Frank Swartz – a panda character orating from a soapbox – was retained on the starboard side.

Frank Swartz was a pilot in the Navy's Torpedo Squadron Five before joining the AVG. He flew in several actions during the Burma battles in early 1942, where he damaged one 'Nate'. He then volunteered to go to Magwe with the Third Squadron after the 'Panda Bears' were rotated to China. On 22 March he was seriously wounded during an air raid there while sharing a slit trench with Crew Chief John Fauth. He was then evacuated to a British military hospital in India. His wounds became infected and he died on 24 April. Fauth had previously died of his wounds as well.

17

Hawk 81-A-2 number '53' (CAF Serial P-8170), assigned to Second Squadron Flight Leader Robert Layher, Rangoon, Burma, January 1942

This machine was flown by many pilots during the intensive Rangoon battles in January and February 1942. 'Tex' Hill scored two victories with it on 24 January and another five days later. The shark head was in the usual pattern, with the eye in white and red. No pilot inscription was carried, and the underwing surfaces had larger than usual Chinese insignia. Its wheel covers were light grey in colour.

18

Hawk 81-A-2 number '57' (CAF serial P-8138), assigned to Second Squadron Vice Leader James H Howard, Kunming, China, May 1942

This aircraft's shark head was in the common style of black, white and red, while the pupils of the eyes were black. The small nose identification numbers were retained, but there was no pilot inscription. The wheel covers were probably painted Dark Earth.

19

Hawk 81-A-2 'photo-ship' (CAF serial probably P-8153), Kunming, China, January 1942

This aeroplane – which was converted for photographic

reconnaissance work in November 1941 – is almost certainly the Tomahawk that Group Photo Officer Erikson Shilling first applied a shark head to. The gaping mouth had blue lips, white teeth and a red tongue, with a thin black or maroon top edge. Note the white 'dimples' and the 'doughnut'-shaped red pupil. Note also the unique white/blue fuselage band – a legacy of this aeroplane's (and Shilling's) earlier attachment to the First, then Second Squadron. By the date illustrated here (mid-January 1942), the large identification number (probably a First Squadron number ending in zero) was painted over. The artist responsible for the 'swami head' marking is unknown, and Shilling has no recollection of it himself. Wheel covers were light grey. This aeroplane was subsequently returned to regular fighter configuration and, with a Disney tiger decal added, assigned an individual number in the seventies.

The modifications necessary to convert this aeroplane to photographic reconnaissance configuration were more extensive than commonly realised. They included removal of the wing guns and cockpit armour, rearrangement of the radio, oxygen and other equipment in the rear fuselage area, and construction of a mounting for the camera in the baggage compartment. A ten-inch opening was cut in the bottom of the fuselage to sight the camera (a Fairchild unit borrowed from Commonwealth forces) through. The gun access and ammunition panels in the wings were also taped over. At the time depicted in profile, the aeroplane's former Second Squadron fuselage identification number was also painted out, making the Tomahawk's special role easily recognisable – yet unadvertised – as it sat on the flightline. Third Squadron armourers Joe Poshefko and Chuck Baisden recall that this aeroplane was 'simonised' by the groundcrew to get a little extra speed, an idea inspired by the smooth finishes seen on crashed Japanese aeroplanes. Some time after mid-April, it was returned to fighter configuration and given an identification number in the seventies. At that time the fighter also received a Disney tiger decal, complete with the light blue 'V-For-Victory' emblem. Frank Schiel also flew some recce missions in this aeroplane, and Ken Jernstedt recalls flying it a few times as well. Some AVG veterans remember that group photographer Joe Pietsker and late-arriving technical wizard Gerhard Neumann ('Herman the German') also assisted Shilling and the groundcrews with this aircraft.

20

Hawk 81-A-2 number '68' (CAF serial P-8109), assigned to Third Squadron Flight Leader Charles Older, Kunming, China, early May 1942

The shark mouth on this aeroplane is representative of the more intricate designs seen on many Third Squadron aeroplanes, featuring unusually thick black lips, white teeth and a red tongue, with the inside of the mouth filled in with a mixed light grey. A thin pink stripe lined the inside edges of both lips and the top of the tongue. The pupil of the eye was red. The markings also included a small inscription near the cockpit, which read *PILOT/C.H.OLDER*, and one of Stanley Regis' red and white 'Hell's Angels' figures (see detail paintings on page 60). It was also adorned with the red/white/blue pinwheels on the wheel covers added in Kunming in January. A Disney 'Flying Tiger' decal was added some time after March 1942. Five kill markings were carried

at this time, but by late May these were replaced with a single line of ten smaller flags. This aeroplane was apparently flown by Robert Hedman on his famous 25 December 'ace in a day' mission, and it was also used by Ken Jernstedt in the 18 March attack on the Japanese airfields at Mudon and Moulmein, with Bill Reed at the controls.

21

Hawk 81-A-2 number '69' (CAF serial P-8115), assigned to Neil Martin and then Lewis Bishop, both from the Third Squadron, Kunming, China, March 1942

This Tomahawk had representative Third Squadron markings, including pinwheels and Stan Regis's red and white 'Hell's Angels' figures. The shark head was in black, red and white, while the area inside the mouth was painted a mixed grey somewhat darker than the underside colour. The eye had a red pupil. No pilot inscription was carried. This fighter was the first Third Squadron machine to sport a 'Hell's Angel' insignia – a simple white line sketch on the rear fuselage applied in September 1941, then removed (see detail painting on page 58). It was flown by Bill Reed during the Third Squadron's baptism of fire over Rangoon on 23 December 1941.

Perhaps this aeroplane was bad luck, for the three pilots most closely associated with it became casualties during their AVG service. The first pilot it was assigned to, Flight Leader Neil Martin, was one of the first two AVG pilots to be killed in action, being apparently hit by a lucky round from a Ki-21 bomber he was attacking on 23 December. Ken Jernstedt, who was following him in the attack, recalls seeing Martin end his run by inexplicably pulling up in front of the bombers, then falling off out of control.

Its next assigned pilot, Vice Squadron Leader Lewis Bishop, had arrived in Burma on 12 November. He saw action in the Christmas Day interception over Rangoon, but was not credited with any victories himself. He helped ferry some Kittyhawks from India in early April 1942, and later that month he was flying ground attack missions in a P-40E, along with pilots of the Second Squadron. On 28 April he was credited with shooting an 'Oscar' off 'Tex' Hill's tail, in addition to one other victory and a probable. On 8 May Bishop participated in attacks against Japanese troops at the Salween River Gorge, and four days later he took part in the AVG attack on the Japanese air base near Hanoi. He was then promoted to Vice Squadron leader, but a few days later, while leading a train-strafing mission in Indochina, he was hit by flak and forced to bail out. He was captured, but in 1945, while being transported to a new PoW camp in Manchuria, he escaped and made his way back to Kunming. Bishop's final victory total with the AVG was 5.20.

The third ill-fated pilot associated with this aeroplane was William 'Black Mac' McGarry, who was shot down in it while flying top cover for a strafing mission on Chiang Mai airfield, in Thailand, on 24 March 1942. He spent the rest of the war as a PoW. In 1990 the wreckage of number '69' was found in a Thai rain forest, and it is now on display at Thai Air Force Base museum at Chiang Mai.

22

Hawk 81-A-2 number '71' (CAF Serial P-8119), assigned to Ed Overend of the Third Squadron, Kunming, China, March 1942

The usual black, white and red elements of the shark head were supplemented by blue filling inside the mouth on this Tomahawk, but with no further detailing. The eye featured the same blue for the pupil, outlined in red. This aeroplane also had Third Squadron pinwheels, a pilot inscription and three kill markings in the usual styles and locations. The exact pattern for the 'Hell's Angels' on this aeroplane is somewhat conjectural, although it was likely similar to the rear view shown here, and certainly placed higher than usual on the fuselage. This aeroplane was wrecked on 10 March 1942.

Edmund Overend frequently flew as Charles Older's wingman, and he participated in the Third Squadron's first combat mission at Rangoon on 23 December. He made many passes on the 'Sallys', and finally got some hits on one straggling Ki-21 and saw it smoking and losing altitude. On 25 December he also attacked the bombers and was credited with destroying two. He was badly hit by return fire or the escorts, however, and had to belly-in. Overend was then posted to Magwe, where he was again forced to crash-land on 7 March. He then went to Loiwing, where he was credited with shooting down a 64th Sentai Ki-43 during the 8 April battle over the airfield. His victim may have been Capt Katsumi Anma, one of the first great pilots lost by the JAAF in the war. He was credited with shooting down another Ki-43 near Lashio on 28 April. Overend had a total of 5.83 victories recognised by CAMCO, and served in the AVG until disbandment. He then rejoined the Marines.

23

Hawk 81-A-2 number '75' (CAF serial P-8186), assigned to Third Squadron Flight Leader William Reed, Kunming, China, January 1942

Like many Third Squadron aeroplanes, this one had two slightly different sets of shark head markings. This was the second one, added in Kunming in January 1942. The shark mouth was in black, white and red, with a thin black stripe just inside the top edge of the tongue and a thin red stripe on the bottom of the upper black lip. Both upper and lower teeth were thinly outlined in black. The mouth was filled with a light grey colour that closely matched the underside camouflage, and the pupil of the eye was painted in concentric rings of red, pink or light grey, and red. The aeroplane had Third Squadron pinwheels and 'Hell's Angel' insignia (see detail painting on page 59). It also featured three kill markings and an inscription near the cockpit that read *PILOT/W.N.REED*. An inscription in the same style was placed on the starboard side, reading *CREW CHIEF/S.REGIS*. Tricolour pinwheels were also added in Kunming. This aircraft was one of a few that originally had an identification number painted under the cockpit, and although this was obscured with with dark green paint, it was still faintly visible underneath.

This fighter's first shark head, which had been applied in Toungoo just prior to the outbreak of hostilities, consisted of black lips, white teeth and a *brown* tongue, with a red stripe on its top edge. The area inside the mouth was also light grey, but only the upper row of teeth was outlined in black. The eye had a probable brown pupil with a thin red edge. The small nose numbers were 'erased' as the aeroplanes were made ready to go to Rangoon, although the port nose number may not have been removed until the fighters were repainted in Kunming.

24

Hawk 81-A-2 number '77' (CAF serial P-8173), assigned to Third Squadron Flight Leader Robert T Smith, Kunming, China, late January 1942

At this time the shark mouth had black lips, white teeth and a red tongue, with the area inside the mouth painted a mixed light grey similar to the undersurface camouflage colour (see close-up view on page 59). The upper row of teeth was thinly outlined in black, and a similar-coloured stripe was placed just inside the top edge of the tongue. The inside edges of the top and bottom lips were thinly lined in red. The eye featured a red pupil, with probably a light grey or pink centre spot. The pilot inscription read *PILOT/R.T.SMITH*. Chinese painters added the red, blue and white pinwheels on the wheel covers, and five white 'meatballs'. This machine also featured a reclining 'Hell's Angel' figure. (see detail view on page 59). Tomahawke '77' was wrecked when the engine failed as 'Dick' Rossi was taking off from Magwe on 23 February 1942. Like other Third Squadron Tomahawks, the colour scheme of the shark head was slightly different when first painted in Toungoo in November-December 1941.

25

Hawk 81-A-2 number '88' (CAF serial P-8121), assigned to Third Squadron Flight Leader Ken Jernstedt, Kunming, China, late January 1942

The shark mouth on this aeroplane was applied in black, red and white, with the inside area filled in with light grey. The upper row of teeth was thinly outlined in black, and the tongue had a thin brown or black edge. The eye had a lighter than usual colour for the pupil – probably light grey, pink or blue. The wheel covers were originally Dark Earth, but red/white/blue pinwheels were added in Kunming in January. The aeroplane carried an inscription under the cockpit, reading *PILOT/K A JERNSTEDT* in smaller than usual letters, with two kill marks underneath. Like several Third Squadron aeroplanes, the original Toungoo shark head colour scheme almost certainly included a brown tongue with a red edge and other detail differences compared to this later one. Note the 'hood ornament' style of 'Hell's Angel' insignia (see 'Hell's Angels' detail paintings on page 59). This aeroplane was destroyed on the ground during a raid on Magwe on 22 March 1942.

26

Hawk 81-A-2 number '92' (CAF serial P-8101), assigned to Third Squadron Flight Leader Robert 'Duke' Hedman, Kunming, China, March 1942

This machine's black, red and white shark mouth was filled with a warm grey colour, and the eyes were white and red. The Third Squadron's tricolour pinwheels were painted on the wheel covers, and a pilot inscription reading *PILOT/DUKE HEDMAN* and five 'meatballs' were located under the cockpit. Hedman's crew chief, Leo J Schramm, recalled that he painted these on right after the pilot's historic Christmas Day victories. This machine had large patches of off-white paint on the lower outer surfaces of the wings, which were probably the result of repairs. According to Schramm, this aeroplane was totally wrecked in a take-off accident at Loiwing involving an intoxicated Greg Boyington in the first few days of April 1942!

27

Hawk 81-A-2 Number '99' (CAF Serial P-8139), assigned to Third Squadron Leader Arvid Olson, Rangoon, Burma, December 1941

Like many Third Squadron aircraft, this aeroplane's original artwork was revised at Kunming in January 1942. These are its first markings, which included a shark mouth with a *brown* tongue and medium blue-grey filling, but apparently no other detailing. The pupil of the eye was the same colour as that inside the mouth. Olson's name was inscribed near the cockpit, and the wheel covers were light grey. The 'Hell's Angels' insignia was incomplete at Rangoon, but this was remedied when the squadron retired to Kunming in January 1942 (see 'Hell's Angels' detail painting on page 59). Note the evidence of overpainted national insignia on the undersurfaces of the wings. At Kunming, the shark head was updated with a red tongue edged in black, while red edging was added to the inside of the upper and lower black lips. The area inside the mouth was repainted in a slightly darker blue-grey, as was the pupil of the eye, which was also thickly outlined in red. The characteristic red, white and blue pinwheels were also added at that time.

28

P-40E-1 Kittyhawk Number '106' (no CAF serial), Loiwing/Baoshan, China, April-May 1942

The somewhat hastily-marked appearance of this Kittyhawk was typical of the ex-USAAF aircraft received by the AVG from late March 1942 onwards. It was finished in standard Dark Olive Drab 41 and Neutral Grey 43 camouflage, with no visible trace of a serial number on the vertical tail surface. AVG personnel obscured the fuselage stars with dark green paint and added Chinese insignia in the usual four positions on the wings, covering the US insignia in the process. The *U.S.ARMY* designators were left on the bottom of the wings, however. The shark mouth was painted in black, white and red, with the camouflage showing inside. The eye was white and black, and Disney 'Flying Tiger' decals were also applied.

COLOUR SECTION

1

The Illustrated Weekly of India for Sunday, 2 November 1941. This 'colourised' illustration of the RAF's No 112 Sqn Tomahawk Is in the Western Desert inspired Charles Bond with the idea of the shark head insignia for the AVG (*Mark Burken*)

2

Third Squadron Flight Leader Robert T Smith and Tomahawk '91' (P-8150) at Kyadaw airfield on Sunday, 23 November 1941. This is the only known colour still photo that documents early Third Squadron shark heads with brown tongues. Note how well the mixed light grey above the tongue – the last colour added by the painter – matches the lower surface camouflage. The painted-over nose number can be faintly seen above the eye. This aeroplane was lost at Rangoon a few weeks after this shot was taken (*R T Smith via Brad Smith*)

3

R T Smith is seen at the Kyadaw airfield 'boneyard' probably on Sunday, 23 November 1941. Tomahawks '74' and '81' had both been wrecked in training accidents a few weeks earlier, but were subsequently 'rehabilitated' by hard-working groundcrews when additional losses made the necessary parts available. Note the disk of green paint under the cockpit of aircraft '74' that covers a misplaced side number (*R T Smith via Brad Smith*)

4

Smith sits in his assigned aircraft, Tomahawk '77', at Kyadaw, again probably on Sunday, 23 November 1941. Note the unfinished 'Hell's Angels' insignia forward of the cockpit (*R T Smith via Brad Smith*)

5

Tomahawk '49' is seen here just after being transferred to the Third Squadron in late April or May 1942, but prior to the addition of new markings by Tom Haywood. Note the starboard camouflage pattern, with provision for the fuselage roundel. Bert Christman's 'orating panda' caricature of Frank Swartz, the original assigned pilot, is also just visible above the wing tip (*R T Smith*)

6

Third Squadron Flight Leader R T Smith poses in the cockpit of Tomahawk '40' at Kunming probably on 23 May 1942. This photo reveals a number of interesting details, including a brown camouflage colour significantly lighter than that seen in colour photos of other AVG Tomahawks (*R T Smith*)

7

The famous Disney 'flying tiger' decals were not received by the AVG until mid-March 1942. R T Smith's jacket has one of Regis' 'Hell's Angels' on it, and his cap sports the Chinese Air Force badge (*R T Smith*)

8

AVG Commander Claire Chennault and Skip Adair of Headquarters Staff are seen at Kunming in May 1942. Adair was probably acting Executive Officer at the time. Note what appears to be a brigadier's star on Chennault's shoulder strap. (*R T Smith via Brad Smith*)

9

Second Squadron Vice Leaders Ed Rector and James Howard, First Squadron Leader Robert Neale, Third Squadron Leader Arvid Olson and Group Adjutant Curtis Smith stop for a portrait outside AVG headquarters at Kunming in May 1942. First Squadron Leader 'Tex' Hill was almost certainly in India when this shot was taken. The occasion for this notable gathering was not recorded, but they were probably assembling to help plan upcoming missions. Meetings like this were rare, since most mission planning was done on a virtually day-to-day basis at squadron level due to the fact that AVG assets were always widely scattered. Olson was a P-40 pilot with the 8th Pursuit Group at Mitchell Field when he signed up for the AVG. When hostilities commenced, Chennault designated him 'Group Commander in the Air', and committed his 'Hell's Angels' to essentially independent

operations at Rangoon. Olson served there in an operational management role, rather than as a leader in the air, largely because communications with group headquarters in Kunming, as well as with RAF units, were a critical problem. Olson proved to be a skilful operational planner, and cautious with limited – and irreplaceable – resources. He began leading operations from the air in January with an escort mission to Indochina, then took charge of AVG operations at Magwe and, later, Loiwing. By that time he was regularly flying patrols with his pilots, and he was credited with shooting down a Ki-43 'Oscar' on 10 April for his only victory. After AVG service, he applied his organisational talents as Operations Officer for the First Air Commando Group, one of the most innovative air combat units ever
(*R T Smith via Brad Smith*)

10

R T Smith poses with Tomahawk '68' at Kunming probably on 23 May 1942. Note the various shades of brown on this heavily weathered aircraft. This is perhaps the AVG's best-known Tomahawk, although its colourful markings had badly weathered by the time these photos were taken (*R T Smith*)

11

Third Squadron aircraft are seen parked at Kunming, probably in May 1942. Visible in this photo are Tomahawks '75', '96', '47', '22' and '35'. Third Squadron fuselage stripes were added as soon as possible to transferred aircraft like numbers '22' and '35', but other 'standard' Third Squadron markings were added only as time and interest permitted. Note what appears to be Neutral Grey under the horizontal stabiliser of Tomahawk '35' (*R T Smith*)

12

Third Squadron pilots pose for R T Smith's camera during a refuelling stop at Yunnan-yi on 28 May 1942. Seated, from left to right, are R T Smith, Ken Jernstedt, Bob Prescott, 'Link' Laughlin and Bill Reed. Standing are Erik Shilling (left) and Squadron Leader Arvid Olson. Not shown is Tom Haywood, who was busy taking the picture! Behind them is Tomahawk '68', flown by Olson on this mission (*R T Smith*)

13

This candid photo was taken at Yunnan-yi on 28 May within minutes of the previous exposure. Chinese workers are using a hand pump to refuel Tomahawk '68' from a drum, while in the foreground more Chinese crewmen work on a primary trainer painted in typical Chinese Air Force green camouflage. (*R T Smith via Brad Smith*)

14

Robert T Smith shot this view from the cockpit of his Tomahawk some time in May 1942. The offset 'iron sights' and the specially built reflector bracket are clearly visible (*R T Smith via Brad Smith*)

15

Third Squadron Tomahawks patrol near the Burma-China border on 28 May 1942. Tomahawk '46' is immediately behind aeroplane '68'. The other aircraft include numbers '49', '24' and '74' (*R T Smith*)

16

This photograph, probably taken in June 1942 at Kunming, is the only known colour still of AVG Kittyhawks
(*R T Smith via Brad Smith*)

17 & 18

Top and bottom views of the right horizontal stabiliser of AVG Tomahawk '69' (Curtiss c/n 15452, P-8115), recovered from the Thai rain forest in 1990 and now on display at the Royal Thai Air Force Base at Chiang Mai (*Dr Ted Brown*)

INDEX

Figures in **bold** refer to illustrations, plates are shown as plate number(s) with caption locators in brackets